Central place theory

Central place theory:
A reinterpretation

Keith S. O. Beavon

Reader in Urban Geography and Associate Professor
of the University of the Witwatersrand, Johannesburg

Longman
London and New York

Longman Group Limited London

Associated companies, branches and representatives
throughout the world

Published in the United States of America
by Longman Inc., New York

First published 1977

Library of Congress Cataloging in Publication Data

Beavon, Keith Sidney Orrock.
    Central place theory.

    Includes bibliographical references.
    1. Central places.   I. Title.
HT159.C44B4   301.36'3   76—42282
ISBN 0 582 48678 5
ISBN 0 582 48683 1 pbk.

Set in IBM Journal 10 on 11pt
and printed in Great Britain by
Whitstable Litho Ltd, Kent

For PAT

Contents

Acknowledgements

We are grateful to the following for permission to reproduce copyright material:

Edward Arnold (Publishers) Ltd for a figure redrawn from Haggett, *Locational Analysis in Human Geography*, 1965; Australian Geographical Studies for a figure redrawn from R. J. Johnston, *Australian Geographical Studies*, 4, 1966; Economic Geography for data from Berry and Garrison, *Economic Geography*, Vol. 34, 1958; Environmental Studies for data from Beavon, *Environmental Studies*, 15, 1975; The Geographical Society of New South Wales for a figure redrawn from P. Scott, *The Australian Geographer*, 9, 1964 © Geographical Society of New South Wales; Geographical Analysis for tables reprinted from 'A Geotaxonomic Approach to Classification in Urban and Regional Studies' by K. S. O. Beavon and A. V. Hall, *Geographical Analysis*, Vol. 4, No. 4 (October 1972). Copyright © 1972 by the Ohio State University Press. Tables and figures reprinted from 'The Lösch System of Market Areas: Derivation and Extension' by K. S. O. Beavon and Alan S. Mabin, *Geographical Analysis*, Vol. 7, No. 2 (April 1975). Copyright © 1975 by the Ohio State University Press. Extracts which originally appeared as 'A Geotaxonomic Approach to Classification in Urban and Regional Studies' by K. S. O. Beavon and A. V. Hall, *Geographical Analysis*, Vol. 4, No. 4 (October 1974) and 'The Lösch System of Market Areas: Derivation and Extension' by K. S. O. Beavon and Alan S. Mabin, *Geographical Analysis*, Vol. 7, No. 2 (April 1975); Gustav Fischer Verlag for figures redrawn from Lösch, *The Economics of Location*, 1954; KNAG Committee for Publications for figures redrawn from Beavon and Mabin, *Tijdschrift voor Economische en Sociale Geografie*, 67, 1976; Northwestern University for a figure redrawn from Garner, *The Internal Structure of Retail Nucleations*, 1966; Prentice-Hall Inc. for figures redrawn from *Central Places in Southern Germany* by Walter Christaller, translated by Carlisle W. Baskin © 1966. Reprinted by permission of Prentice-Hall Inc.; South African Geographical Society for data redrawn from K. S. O. Beavon, *South African Geographical Journal*, Vols 52, 54, 56 and 57; South African Geographical Journal for a figure redrawn from R. J. Davies, *South African Geographical Journal*, 49, 1967; University of Chicago for tables redrawn from Berry, *Commercial Structure and Commercial Blight*, 1963, and a figure redrawn from Barnum, *Service Centres in Baden Wurtemberg*, 1966; University of Otago for a figure redrawn from L. J. King, The Proceedings of the *Third New Zealand Geographical Conference*, 1962; University of Pennsylvania for figures redrawn from Rushton, *Papers of the Regional Science Association*, 28, 1972, and from Berry and Garrison, *Papers and Proceedings of the Regional Science Association*, 4, 1958c.

Preface

August Lösch wrote *Die räumliche Ordnung der Wirtschaft* in 1939. Contained therein are ideas on market areas that hold the key to the meaningful understanding of the location of intra-urban tertiary activities. Notwithstanding, his work was ignored by geographers at the time that central place theory was being extended to the intra-urban scale in 1958. The fact that Lösch's work was apparently rejected appears to be the result of a misinterpretation of a section of his book. Certainly the work is difficult to read, and this difficulty has been compounded by the lack of an explicit statement by Lösch on the method used for deriving his market systems and resultant hierarchical system of market centres. Editorial errors in the explanatory notes inserted in the book after his death in 1945 have only added to the confusion.

By contrast it is easier to understand the central place system of Christaller and its extension into the theory of tertiary activity. The net result is that geographers seeking a model to provide a meaningful conceptual basis for understanding the system of central places at both the inter- and intra-urban scales have been led to follow the ideas of Christaller's classic central place theory and the subsequent theory of tertiary activity as expounded by Berry and Garrison.

Possibly because both classic central place theory and the theory of tertiary activity postulate stepped and clearly definable hierarchies, much research effort has been expended in seeking and establishing such hierarchies. This effort has continued over a long period despite observations suggesting that central places may be arranged along a continuum rather than in a stepped hierarchy. No theoretical basis for the continuum has been advanced.

In this book an attempt is made to provide the theoretical basis for a continuum of central places at the intra-urban scale. In order to achieve this it is necessary to reconcile apparent differences between classic central place theory and the theory of tertiary activity; to examine *a priori* the Löschian system of market areas and market centres; and thereby to develop a model of the location of intra-metropolitan tertiary activities.

The book falls essentially into two parts. In the first, extending over five chapters, the early work on central place theory following on the work of Christaller and leading to the formulation of the theory of tertiary activity is examined in some detail. A re-examination of the work of Christaller then follows and it is shown that discrepancies exist between the interpretations that have been made of Christaller's work and the original work. The techniques that have been adopted for empirically determining hierarchies are next reviewed. A case study of Cape Town, in which a geotaxonomic approach to classification has been used, is discussed in some detail as it was that study that led the author to search for an alternative central place model that would account for an intra-urban continuum of tertiary nucleations. The second part of the book is concerned with the latter model and commences with a re-examination of the work of Lösch which is then extended to provide the relevant theoretical approach.

In 1962 I happened to meet with my former mentor David Hywel Davies in Holland. Over a cup of coffee I expressed my interest in getting to grips with something of interest in the newly expanding field of urban geography. He replied that the works of Christaller and Lösch appeared to be arousing some interest and recommended that I investigate them further. This book has grown out of that initial spark which fired my interest. It has also grown out of the freedom I have enjoyed to experiment in both the teaching and research areas of central place theory at the University of the Witwatersrand.

Having now taught the content of this book to undergraduates for the last three years or so, it is possible to make some comments about how classes of similar students elsewhere may be able to use it. Naturally how the material is incorporated depends on how courses are structured at various universities. At the University of the Witwatersrand students take short courses in central place studies in each of the three undergraduate years. On the assumption that the central place theory of Christaller is poorly taught in high schools, if at all, it has been incorporated in the first-year course. Much of the material contained here in Chapter 3 is then presented. Depending on the ability of the class it has sometimes been necessary to proceed no further than the discussion of Fig. 3.16. Indeed, the latter portion of Chapter 3 is best discussed with students after they have been exposed to the discussion of the theory of tertiary activity that is contained in Chapter 2. At the University of the Witwatersrand the content of Chapter 2 and much of Chapter 4 is handled with second year students. The latter chapter, dealing with scattergrams and classification, can be incorporated with the practical classes. At the third year of the undergraduate programme the derivation of the Löschian system, its expansion into an intra-urban model, and the generalisation of that model is taught. For this it has been found that students do need constant access to the diagrams contained in Chapters 6, 7 and 8. At the Honours level, i.e. in the fourth year of specialised study that constitutes a postgraduate course at South African universities, the work is used as a starting point and as a new framework for examining the more theoretical aspects of the literature on rank-size and central place relationships, and certain aspects of the developing area of behaviouralism and space-preference structures.

During the course of the last few years much of the material included in the book has been published in the form of journal papers. I am grateful to the editors of *The South African Geographical Journal, Geographical Analysis* and the occasional paper series of the University of the Witwatersrand entitled *Environmental Studies* for allowing me to draw heavily on material first published with them.

A number of persons have offered advice and constructive criticism of the work as it progressed. Among my colleagues at Wits I wish to thank Peter Tyson and Denis Fair for their continued interest and offers of constructive criticism. Also to Aarnt Spandau of the same University and Anthony Hall, Geoff Brundrit and Ben Gurzynski of the University of Cape Town who did much to assist me. The illustrations were prepared by members of the Cartographic Section of the Geography Department. In particular I wish to thank Philip Stickler, Ian Conochie and Jenny Rouse. I also wish to acknowledge financial support from the Universities of Cape

Town and the Witwatersrand, as well as from the Human Sciences Research Council in Pretoria. Naturally, any shortcomings of the book remain the sole responsibility of the author.

I owe a particularly great debt of gratitude to a small group of people who were Honours students and research students at Wits during the time that I needed a sounding-board most. In Alan Mabin, Chris Rogerson, Gordon Pirie, Keyan Tomaselli, Lyn Ross, Ethel Beardall, Barbara Boden and Harry Tate. I found the stimulus of inquiring minds, the arguments, and sharp retorts so essential to academic debate. Their feedback into my work has considerably enhanced whatever clarity it might now have for undergraduates. I hope that these former Honours students of mine gained as much as I did from the experience. Certainly the sheer pleasure that came from the many light-hearted and sometimes hilarious moments that accompanied the different stages of this work have alone made the effort worthwhile.

Only those who have written a book can really appreciate the assistance given by a wife who takes all the cares of the family and the home on her own shoulders and copes. To my wife Pat goes my greatest thanks.

Johannesburg, Autumn 1976 KEITH BEAVON

'Lösch's work opens up new vistas and new avenues of research'

Wolfgang F. Stolper

Chapter 1

Introduction

The object of this book is to present the development of a conceptual model of the location of intra-metropolitan tertiary activity and to put it forward as an alternative to the model derived from the present theory of tertiary activity. As such it follows suggestions by Stolper (1955), Dacey (1965b), Yeates and Garner (1971) and Parr (1973) that the Lösch system of markets should be extended to the intra-urban level. The key to the understanding of the intra-metropolitan system of tertiary activity is contained in the section of Lösch's *Economics of Location* (1954) dealing with networks of market areas and systems of networks. To grasp the full relevance of Lösch's ideas on marketing as the basis for the meaningful understanding of intra-urban locations of tertiary activities, it is necessary to re-examine *a priori* the principles and propositions set out in *The Economics of Location*. In offering an alternative model to that currently subscribed to and based on the theory of tertiary activity it is first necessary to show why such an alternative should be considered at all.

It is generally accepted among geographers that central place theory constitutes a deductive base for the understanding of the real world patterns of the location and operation of retail and service businesses. Furthermore it has been suggested that central place theory (i.e., theory relating to the regularity in size, composition and distribution of those urban places primarily serving their hinterlands) constitutes a strong deductive base for the formulation of a theory of tertiary activity (i.e., an extension of central place theory to include the intra-urban system of shopping centres). Much work in theoretical urban geography, and many empirical studies in both urban geography, and urban and regional planning, rest on these theories and attest to the zeal and enthusiasm with which they have been applied. Careful examination of the basic tenets and assumptions of the theories and their associated models reveals, however, that much of the confidence with which they have been applied may well be ill-founded.

Integral to both theories is a stepped hierarchy of central places. It will be contended in this book that such hierarchies have been recognised more readily than is justifiable on empirical grounds and the notion of a stepped hierarchy must be rejected. Instead the postulation of continua at the inter- and intra-urban scales appears to be both a logical and empirical necessity.

In setting out to provide an alternative model of the intra-metropolitan location of tertiary activity that accords more closely with reality than does the stepped hierarchical model, it will be shown that the theory of tertiary activity is less of an extension of classic central place theory than has been claimed.

As Carter (1972) has stated, no consideration of central place theory can proceed far without reference to Christaller's seminal theory. For although it is built upon earlier ideas and studies, Walter Christaller's classic work *Die zentralen Orte in Süddeutschland* is generally regarded as the precursor of all subsequent attempts to understand the nature of order in central place systems. First published in German in 1933 it was only some ten years later that the ideas it contained began to reach geographers in the English-speaking world. By 1957 a microfilm of Baskin's English translation was available, but it is doubtful that it was read widely. Only in 1966 was *Die zentralen Orte in Süddeutschland* freely available in the English version, *Central Places in Southern Germany*. However, between 1957 and 1966 a number of important papers were published by Berry and Garrison (1958a, b, c). These papers dealt with theoretical aspects of Christaller's work, empirical verification, and the extension of central place theory into a more general theory of tertiary activity. One of these papers, that dealing with developments in central place theory (Berry and Garrison, 1958c), is particularly important. It provides the basis for asserting that in broad terms central place theory is more applicable to intra-urban than to inter-urban central place systems as originally conceived by Christaller. The paper just referred to drew attention for the need to recognise two fundamental components of central place systems, viz., the structural and behavioural. It is the stepped hierarchy of the structural component, and not the hexagonal market areas associated with the behavioural component, that is the most characteristic feature of the Christaller system of central places. Likewise in the theory of tertiary activity it is again the stepped hierarchy that is the most characteristic feature.

Controversy exists concerning the validity of the theories that postulate stepped hierarchies of central places. Many empirical studies have examined systems of central places at both the inter- and intra-urban scales and have identified hierarchies that accord well with those postulated by both classic central place theory and the theory of tertiary activity[1].* Studies of consumer movement patterns, although fewer in number, have cast doubt on the validity of the implied behavioural aspects of the theory of tertiary activity. Nonetheless, as evidenced by continuous direct and indirect references to it in the growing volume of textbooks on urban geography, the theory of tertiary activity remains the single generally accepted theory of intra-urban central place systems, if not of all central place systems[2].

Probably because the development and propagation of the theory of tertiary activity in 1958 pre-dated the publication of Baskin's translation in 1966, geographers failed to examine that document as carefully as they might. By 1966 many geographers appear to have subscribed to the viewpoint that central place theory was based on unnecessarily restrictive assumptions that precluded an interpretation that would serve as a model for understanding a central place system in which excess profits were found. It is accepted here that Baskin's (1966) translation of Christaller's study, *Central Places in Southern Germany*, is accurate in both detail and sense, and that it is in no way different in these respects from his microfilmed translation (1957). From a re-examination of what is essentially Christaller's original work it appears that the *interpretation* of Christaller, as presented subsequent to 1957, is both partially incorrect and incomplete. It has been argued (Beavon, 1975) that the ideas of Christaller, if fully interpreted, negate the claims that the theory of tertiary activity represents an extension of Christaller's theory.

It is most important, however, to bear in mind the status of the discipline and

* Numbers in [square brackets] indicate Notes at end of the chapter.

the associated intellectual climate that prevailed in the late 1950s and early 1960s, and not to condemn the work of any particular researcher. Geography as a discipline was becoming involved in what has since been called the quantitative revolution. This was in many ways a traumatic period for those involved in the discipline as Burton's (1963) account ably demonstrates. It gave rise to a great flurry of quantitative work with increasing emphasis on the development of abstract and mathematical models. Although Christaller had written his treatise in 1933, and although it had been read at least in part by some geographers outside Europe by 1940, its wider dissemination was apparently curtailed by the holocaust of the Second World War. As such many geographers probably first encountered Christaller's work not through the efforts of Carlisle Baskin (1957), but through the papers that appeared in the interim period 1957−65 before Carlisle's translation was published. Bear in mind too that this was a period when the quantitative revolution was gaining its momentum in human geography. Thus the geometric precision, mathematical flavour, and deductive properties of central place theory were obviously pleasing to many young geographers who were to carry the revolution forward. That it can only now be contended that misinterpretations of Christaller, and Lösch, occurred in 1958 gives some measure of the stature of those early front-runners who carried human geography out of its floundering age of description.

However, because of the misinterpretation a large number of the studies, of both inter- and intra-urban central place systems that have followed since 1958, have been based almost entirely on the theory of tertiary activity enunciated in 1958. It appears appropriate therefore to commence this book with a review of the theory of tertiary activity. This in turn will facilitate a meaningful base for the re-examination of Christaller's work. Whereas this book is principally concerned with developing an alternative model for the intra-urban central place system, it is never-theless necessary at the outset to consider both inter- and intra-urban systems as reported in the literature.

The relevant field of literature is not only voluminous but it is wide ranging and covers many different facets of central place study. The numerous papers that have been published in this field of geography have been compiled into three bibli-ographies. The earliest includes about 1,000 references (Berry and Pred, 1961); the two subsequent collections of references (Barnum, Kasperson and Kiuchi, 1965; Andrews, 1970) list appoximately 350 and 300 studies respectively. It appears reasonable to suppose that the total literature now encompasses some 2,000 papers.

Naturally not all the literature is concerned with the statements of central place theory *per se*. Nor are the majority of the papers primarily concerned with the verification and application of the theory. Encompassed in the field of central place studies are papers concerned mainly with such diverse focii of interest as the charac-teristics of service areas of medical services, the nature of planned shopping centres and the delimitation of the central business district. Nevertheless there are suf-ficient publications concerned primarily with the theoretical foundations of the field, and with the verification and application of central place theory to preclude meaningful discussion of them all. In the chapter that follows the author has selected those papers that he regards as the essential stepping stones along which so many geographers have followed. Stepping stones that took the work of Christaller from a research frontier to its niche in many introductory courses in human geography today. That the selection is a personal selection cannot be denied. Whether it is a meaningful selection that correctly justifies the alternative model, a hybrid of essentially Löschian ideas, spiced with ideas borrowed from both Christaller's central place theory and Berry and Garrison's theory of tertiary activity, is for the reader to decide. Furthermore the discussion that follows is concerned almost exclusively with the structural components of central place theory and central place systems. The behavioural components are examined only in passing. This is not to imply that the latter components are not important. On the contrary, it is suggested that they are so important as to constitute a research frontier at the present time. However, the incorporation of such ideas, as manifest in the space-preference approach to behaviour, must first await the verdict on the structural components of the intra-metropolitan model of the location of tertiary activity enunciated here.

Notes

1. *Inter alia*: in North America — Canoyer, 1946; Ratcliff, 1949; Garrison, 1950; Brush, 1953; Brush and Bracey, 1955; Berry and Garrison 1958a; Garrison *et al.*, 1959; Berry, Barnum and Tennant, 1962; Berry, 1963; Simmons, 1964, 1966; Garner, 1966; Berry, 1967; Marshall, 1969: in Britain — Smailes, 1944; Bracey, 1953; Carruthers, 1962; Lomas, 1964; Davies, W., 1967; Lewis, 1970; Rowley, 1970: in New Zealand — King, 1962; Clark, W., 1967: in Australia — Scott, 1964; Johnston, 1966: in Africa — Carol, 1952; Abiodun, 1967; Davies, R. J., 1967; Davies and Cook, 1968: in Europe — Palomäki, 1964; Barnum, 1966; Vrišer, 1971.
2. Berry, 1967; Johnson, 1967; Thoman, Conkling and Yeates, 1968; Berry and Horton, 1970; Leahy, McKee and Dean, 1970; Morrill, 1970; Abler, Adams and Gould, 1971; Bourne, 1971; Yeates and Garner, 1971; Carter, 1972; Everson and FitzGerald, 1972; Goodall, B., 1972; Lloyd and Dicken, 1972.

Chapter 2

The theory of tertiary activity: a critical assessment

As indicated in the Introduction, this chapter will review a selection of the relevant literature concerned with both the inter-urban and intra-urban tertiary systems and their role in the development of the theory of tertiary activity.

The inter-urban hierarchy

Early developments

Despite Christaller's use of a homogeneous transport surface to reduce the vagaries of spatial reality, it appears that the actual presence of such a surface was seen by some as a necessary prerequisite for order in a settlement system (Berry and Pred, 1961, p. 5). The tenure of this viewpoint extends to at least 1960 (e.g., by Curry, 1962, p. 32). Thus it is not surprising that two of the early studies that set out to examine aspects of central place theory empirically (Carol, 1952; Brush, 1953) were conducted in areas closely approximating the ideal conditions (Brush, 1953, p. 330). However, similar studies conducted in the mid-1940s and early 1950s are not overtly concerned with the apparently restrictive nature of Christaller's implied assumptions (e.g., Smailes, 1944; Bracey, 1953). The early 1950s also mark the appearance of the first major comparative study of central place systems in different regions (Brush and Bracey, 1955) and the attempts to reconstruct the urban hierarchy of a past period (Carter, 1956).

Towards the end of the 1950s three major[1] papers concerned with both the theory and empirical study of central places appeared (Berry and Garrison, 1958a, b, c); the first replied to the stinging criticism that Vining (1955) had levelled at Brush's (1953) now classic study of central places in Wisconsin. In criticising the three-step hierarchy that had been identified in Wisconsin, Vining implied that central places were differentiated along a continuum rather than in a stepped hierarchy. This implication, if it had been left unchallenged, could have seriously undermined central place theory, regarded in 1958 as 'geography's finest intellectual product' (Bunge, 1962, p. 129). The bench-mark study of central places in Snohomish County, Washington (Berry and Garrison, 1958a), set out to provide empirical evidence for the existence of a hierarchical system of urban centres. The study was more carefully structured in terms of the requirements necessary to verify the *theoretical findings* of Christaller than earlier studies had been. Particular attention was paid to the theoretical requirement that a hierarchical central place system should have two essential characteristics — the first explicit and the second implicit. Explicitly, each order (or class) of town possesses discrete central activities and, implicitly, is characterised by a specific population size. It follows from the theory that orders of towns with more complex sets of activities will possess all the central activities of lower orders plus a group of central activities that will distinguish them from the central places of immediately lower order. Thus, because central places theoretically have discrete groups of activities, and because they are believed to have specific populations it was argued that it should be possible to differentiate a set of central places into hierarchical orders on the basis of either the number of central activities, or people, in each town (Berry and Garrison, 1958a, p. 147).

Establishing the hierarchy

In the Snohomish County study (Berry and Garrison, 1958a), data for thirty-three central places was classified into fifty-two categories of central activity and ranked with respect to population size and number of central activities. Making use of the Clark and Evans (1954) definition of a group, viz., that every member of a group should be closer to a member of the group than to any other member, three groups of central place, A, B and C, were identified (Fig. 2.1).

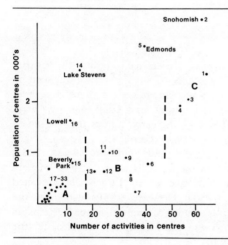

Fig. 2.1 Groups of central places in Snohomish County. The places are numbered to allow for comparison with the dendrograms presented in Chapter 4 (after Berry and Garrison, *Econ. Geog.*, 34, 1958a).

It was also suggested (Berry and Garrison, 1958a, p. 149), that the population of an urban centre could be specified as a function of the number of business firms of each type of business. This was in accordance with Christaller's suggestion that through the working of the income mechanism the population of a central place is a function of the number and types of central commodities and services it provides. For each of the fifty-two categories of business for which data was available in the Snohomish study regression lines based on equations of the form

$$P = A(B^N) \tag{2.1}$$

where P is population and N number of businesses, were determined. The constants A and B were empirically derived for each business type. Justification for this particular form of exponential function was not given. Calculation of the apparent threshold population for each type of business was determined by setting N to unity[2]. Groups of *variates*, business types that occur in variable numbers, were

Table 2.1 Number of businesses per central business type per central place in the groups of business types and central places in Snohomish County, Washington (after Berry and Garrison, *Econ. Geog.*, 34, 1958a).

Central business types	Order of central places		
	(*Low*) ← A	B	C → (*High*)
Groups of variates			
(*Low order*)			
1_1	0.65	2.91	6.29
2_1	0.04	0.77	2.65
3_1	0.01	0.21	1.00†
(*High order*)			
Groups of attributes			
(*Low order*)			
General store	0.70	0.11	0.00
1_2	0.20	0.45	1.00†
2_2	0.04	0.50	1.00†
3_2	0.03	0.28	0.88
(*High order*)			

† A value of 1.00 means that every place of a particular class will tend to have one business of each type found in the group of attributes or variates (e.g., Order C places have one business in each of the business types of group 2_2).

established on the basis of their ranked threshold values; three groups of variates were found in Snohomish County. *Attributes*, central business types that are either present or absent, were grouped on the basis of their ranked point-biserial correlations between population and business type. Again three groups were found (Table 2.1).

It was then argued that the overall pattern of central business types and central places can be seen more readily when the results in Table 2.1 are generalised and presented symbolically as in Table 2.2, where the step-like hierarchical structure is emphasised.

Table 2.2 Orders of central places and associated groupings of central business types in Snohomish County (after Berry and Garrison, op. cit., 34, 1958a).

Central business types	Order of central places		
	(*Low*) ← A†	B	C → (*High*)
Groups of variates			
(*Low order*)			
1_1	p	c	c
2_1	—	p	c
3_1	—	s	c
(*High order*)			
Groups of attributes			
(*Low order*)			
General store	p	—	—
1_2	s	p	c
2_2	—	p	c
3_2	—	s	p
(*High order*)			

s = some; p = partially; c = complete.

† The Order A place, for example, provides a partial selection of the business types of group 1_1 and some of the business types of group 1_2.

The results of the Snohomish study suggested, first, that a step-like progression in the provision of central business types did occur as the order of the central place increased. Secondly, the evidence suggested that the three classes of towns identified did have discrete levels of population. The combined result thus tended to support the assertion that a central place system of the type deduced from Christallerian theory did in fact exist. However, the deviant cases of Beverly Park, Lowell, Lake Stevens, Edmonds, and Snohomish (Fig. 2.1) were only noted.

It is important to note that the Snohomish study *set out* to show that a stepped hierarchy *did* exist. The study did not set out to examine *whether* a stepped hierarchy *might* exist. In achieving the objective it had set itself, the study introduced the concept of threshold population as the basis for grouping of central activities. Since then the easily calculated threshold populations have played a more important role in determining central place hierarchies than the strictly more appropriate, but less tractable, outer limit of the range of a business type. It appears that the use of threshold populations in this case has been more expedient than necessarily desirable.

The relationship between number of businesses and population is further examined in the second of the set of three bench-mark papers (Berry and Garrison, 1958b). However, it is in the third paper (Berry and Garrison, 1958c) that the theory of tertiary activity is presented. It is this theory that currently remains the only general theory of tertiary activity in geography. Unfortunately, as will be shown in the re-presentation below, the theory of tertiary activity springs from what now appears to be an incorrect interpretation of Christaller, and fails to incorporate the ideas of Lösch (1954)[3]. Furthermore, what has appeared to many to be the most appealing aspect of the theory of tertiary activity, namely the derivation of a stepped hierarchy without prior assumptions about uniform distributions of population, is now suspect, having been seriously questioned by Johnston (1966) and Marshall (1969).

The theoretical foundations

It is in the apparent belief that Christaller's central place theory rested on a homogeneous distribution of purchasing power and on the apparent impression that excess profits are excluded, that an attempt was made in 1958 to reformulate central place theory (see Berry and Garrison, 1958c). It was the express intention to do so without the limiting assumptions of a uniform distribution of purchasing power and without a normal-profits-only style of operation. The argument is based on Christaller's concepts of an outer and inner limit of the range of a commodity, which are now termed *the range* and *threshold* respectively. From this base it is argued that not only can a stepped hierarchy of central places be derived but excess profits will be part of the system.

There are two components to the theory of tertiary activity; one relates to the hierarchical structure and profit situations, and is explicit in the theory; the second component concerns the behaviour of consumers, and is implicit. These two components can now be considered.

The explicit or structural component
In the theory of tertiary activity it is assumed that an area is to be supplied with n types of central commodities[4]. These commodities are ranked from 1 to n in

ascending order of *threshold requirements*. The central place supplying commodity n will require the largest amount of purchasing power to support it. The central place that supplies commodity n is termed an A centre. There will be as many A centres as there are unit threshold sales levels to support firms supplying commodity n. Commodities with lower threshold requirements, e.g., $n - 1, n - 2$, etc., can now be offered from A centres, and at all these centres excess profits may be earned. In terms of efficiency B centres will emerge to also offer a commodity $n - i$, if the interstitial purchasing power located between A centres that also offer commodity $n - i$, exactly equals the threshold requirements for that commodity. Under these circumstances only normal profits can be earned on commodity $n - i$ at both A and B centres, but excess profits may be earned on commodities $n - (i + 1)$, $n - (i + 2)$, etc. Commodities n and $n - i$ are termed marginal hierarchical commodities as they introduce new levels in the hierarchy of shopping centres and only normal profits are possible. The same is true for commodities $n - j$, $n - k$, etc., where $i < j < k$ (Table 2.3). For all other commodities it is possible to earn excess profits.

Table 2.3   The supply of n commodities (goods) by M shopping centres. Marginal hierarchical commodities are indicated by an asterisk and x indicates the set of commodities supplied by the centre (after Berry and Garrison, *Pap. Proc. Reg. Sci.*, 4, 1958c).

Centres	Commodities				
	$n^*, n - 1, \ldots$	$(n-i)^*, n - (i + 1), \ldots$	$(n-j)^*, n - (j + 1), \ldots$	$\ldots$	$k^*, (k - 1), \ldots, 2, 1,$
A	x	x	x	$\ldots$	x
B		x	x	$\ldots$	x
C			x	$\ldots$	x
.				$\ldots$	$\ldots$
.				$\ldots$	$\ldots$
.				$\ldots$	$\ldots$
M				$\ldots$	x

All places of any particular order (other than the lowest) possess all the activities or commodities of the lower order places and in addition possess certain activities that characterise the central place as a higher order place. Not only is this structural aspect explicit in the theory but so is the distinction between marginal hierarchical commodities (or business types), that may earn no more than normal profits, and other commodities (or business types) that may earn excess profits.

The implicit or behavioural component

Garner's (1966) interpretation of the theory of tertiary activity introduces the behavioural component of tertiary activity theory. In his study (Garner, 1966, pp. 14–16) four major implications that can be drawn from the theory of tertiary activity are recognised:

1. *Lower order business centres offer only low order commodities and serve tributary areas defined by the lowest range marginal hierarchical commodity. Low level commodities are generally necessities that are consequently purchased frequently, and correspond to what have been termed* convenience goods *in the planning literature.*
2. *High order business centres provide not only high order commodities that require higher thresholds but all lower order commodities as well. High order*

commodities correspond to shopping goods *of the planning literature. Consumers are prepared to travel greater distances, albeit less frequently, to purchase their commodities.*

3. *Business centres at any level in the hierarchy will offer more commodities, have more businesses, more business types and serve larger tributary areas and tributary populations and have greater total sales volumes than any business centre of a lower level.*

4. *Given the relationships set out above, a complex pattern of nested trade areas results and any consumer is served most efficiently by the closest and most accessible business centre accordant with the commodity required.*

The above interpretation of the behavioural aspects of the theory of tertiary activity took into account the stepped hierarchical arrangement of shopping centres. It also recognised the distinction that existed between consumer usage of convenience retailers and retailers dealing in commodities that evoked comparative shopping. These latter retailers may also be termed 'shopping' retailers.

Re-examination of the theory of tertiary activity

Despite the general acceptance that a stepped hierarchy occurs regardless of the distribution of purchasing power, this aspect of the theory of tertiary activity deserves closer examination. It appears perfectly reasonable and correct for A centres to emerge under these relaxed assumptions and to offer all commodities, from the commodity with the highest threshold requirement down to that with the lowest threshold requirement. The emergence of B centres and other lower order centres depends on the amount of purchasing power interstitial between the A centres. It is apparent from the theory as set out above, and summarised in Table 2.3, that all B centres will be identical in terms of the variety of commodities offered. Furthermore, each level of lower order centre will be identical in terms of the variety of commodities offered. However, only if there is an equal amount of purchasing power in the interstitial areas between A centres, and similarly between successively lower order centres, will it be logical to expect each B centre, each C centre, etc., to offer exactly the same variety of central commodities and to obtain the same variety of central business types as all other A, B, C, centres, etc. As indicated, it has been argued elsewhere (Johnston, 1966, p. 33; Marshall, 1969, p. 34) that it is implicit in the theory of tertiary activity that the amounts of purchasing power in the interstitial areas be approximately equal in order for the stepped hierarchy to appear. It would appear that the equal distribution of purchasing power in the interstitial areas is a necessary constraint. It must be accepted that the need for an even distribution of interstitial purchasing power was not foreseen when the theory of tertiary activity was formulated. Furthermore, it appears that the work of Christaller had not then been examined in the general manner, nor in terms of both excess and normal profits situations, as it will be in Chapter 3 of this book. This being the case, the derivation of the theory of tertiary activity with its stepped hierarchy and with the system of central places capable of earning both normal and excess profits, must have appeared very different from the original presentation by Christaller of a central place system with hexagonal market areas. Consequently, the claim (Berry and Garrison, 1958c) that the theory of tertiary activity represents an extension of central place theory must be seen as having been valid in 1958[5].

Lösch excluded

In extending central place theory to a theory of tertiary activity (Berry and Garrison, 1958c), the work of Lösch (1954) was excluded due, it is believed, to an erroneous interpretation of Lösch's work (Beavon, 1974a). In the brief summary of the contribution of Lösch to central place theory, the 1958 paper (Berry and Garrison, 1958c, pp. 109—10) makes the incorrect statement that the Löschian approach excluded the possibility of a firm earning excess profits. This statement coupled with the apparent difficulty of constructing the Lösch system of market networks probably accounts for his work having been almost completely ignored in the subsequent theoretical developments in the field of central place studies.

The intra-urban hierarchy

Whereas the original system of central places (Christaller, 1966) is concerned with central places on an inter-city scale, it has been claimed that the hierarchy of central places associated with the theory of tertiary activity accords closely with the intra-urban system of central places, i.e., shopping centres (Berry and Garrison, 1958c, p. 113).

Early empirical observations

An understanding of the location and spatial relationships of different kinds of business types and the commercial structure of cities has accumulated over a number of years through a series of empirical studies (see Berry and Pred, 1961, Section VI, pp. 65—72). Among the most important definitive studies that have had an influence on the intra-urban expression of the theory of tertiary activity are investigations of American cities by Rolph (1929), Proudfoot (1937), Canoyer (1946), Ratcliff (1949), and Garrison (1950). These are discussed in turn below.

The study of Baltimore (Rolph, 1929) is among the first of the intensive investigations of the nature of the commercial structure of cities. Five types of business areas are recognised: a central business district, retail sub-centres, string streets, neighbourhood facility groups and non-concentrated business. The types of activities associated with each are also enumerated.

Observations of nine large American cities including Philadelphia and Chicago confirm the five-rank hierarchy identified by Rolph (Proudfoot, 1937), albeit in a modified terminology that may have anticipated the later work by Canoyer (1946) and Ratcliff (1949). The five types of business areas recognised are: a central business district, outlying business centres, principal business thoroughfares, neighbourhood business streets and isolated store clusters.

Canoyer (1946) introduces the notion that there are two basic types of commercial areas, viz., cluster types or nucleations, and strings or ribbon developments. The nucleations include the central business district, community shopping district and neighbourhood centre.

On the basis of studies in Detroit and elsewhere Ratcliff suggests that outside of the central business district, the outlying business structure is composed of variations and combinations of two basic conformations: business nucleations of which there are two grades or levels, and string street developments (Ratcliff, 1949).

On the basis of a pre-1940 classification of community business centre, major and minor neighbourhood business centres, principal business thoroughfares, and isolated businesses, Garrison (1950) provides detailed information of both the type of business characterising each type of centre and the size and spacing of centres.

The studies of the internal nature of business areas of cities by the middle of this century resemble closely the studies that had been conducted on an inter-city level. It is not surprising therefore that attempts have been made to verify empirically the occurrence of intra-urban hierarchies of business activities in shopping centres (Garrison et al., 1959).

Establishing a type hierarchy

The initial empirical study designed to *establish* the *type* intra-urban hierarchy (Garrison et al., 1959) was based on the city of Spokane (population at the time 185,000). The procedure adopted involved the calculation of a correlation matrix (using the Pearson product—moment correlation) to estimate the spatial association of each pair of forty-nine business types in the 285 business centres identified in the city. On the basis of the resulting correlation matrix, spatially proximate business types were grouped using a linkage analysis technique (McQuitty, 1957) and the same definition of a group (Clark and Evans, 1954) as employed in the Snohomish County study (Berry and Garrison, 1958a). For the groups so identified, the correlation procedure was repeated to establish whether groups of proximate business types themselves had distinctive patterns of association. Two distinctive conformations emerged — nucleated and arterial-road groups. Following on this procedure 'average centres' (Garrison et al., 1959, p. 76) were computed to be representative of business centres with only one, two, three, four, five, etc., business types. The same procedure of correlation and linkage was re-applied and a grouping of average centres into four classes emerged. A similar analysis was conducted for the arterial-type centres.

Comparison of the results from Spokane with the three cities of Cedar Rapids (population c. 90,000), Phoenix (population c. 185,000) and Cincinnati (population c. 370,000), together with the results of other studies (Berry, 1962) leads to the conclusion that the intra-urban commercial structure in general consists of four basic components. These presented in a modified form (by Berry, 1963, p. 19) are:

1. Isolated convenience stores and street-corner developments;
2. Neighbourhood business centres;
3. Community business centres; and
4. Regional shopping centres.

The relationship between the nucleated business centres, the ribbons and other specialised areas is shown in Fig. 2.2.

Theoretical rationale

The intra-urban hierarchy that has been recognised for the American city is based on empirical evidence. However, the *a priori* argument used in deriving the stepped hierarchy of tertiary activities (Berry and Garrison, 1958c) has also been used to provide the theoretical rationale for the intra-urban hierarchy (Berry, 1963, pp. 113—15). By simply commencing with an assumed population in a metropolitan area, an intra-urban hierarchy can be shown to emerge in the same manner as an inter-urban hierarchy (Table 2.4). Further theoretical justification for the resultant hierarchic model has been provided (Berry, 1963, pp. 112—16), by

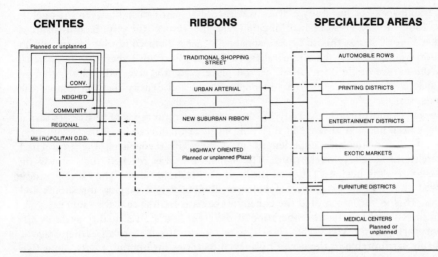

Fig. 2.2 The intra-urban hierarchy and commercial structure of American cities (after Berry, *Commercial Structure and Commercial Blight*, 1963).

showing the conformity between it and Baumol and Ide's (1956) model of consumer behaviour.

By 1963, the theory of tertiary activity had been shown to be applicable to both the inter- and intra-urban levels. Furthermore, it was shown to accord well with the results of earlier empirical investigations. Additional empirical studies of the North American and other cities followed (*inter alia* Simmons, 1964 and 1966; Garner, 1966; Johnston, 1966) in which hierarchies were identified largely on the basis of the 'key' provided by Berry's (1963) study of Chicago. Certain shortcomings now become apparent.

Critical variations

The study of Chicago in 1966 (Garner, 1966) is particularly important. Unfortunately the queries raised by Garner do not appear to have had the exposure they deserve. His study questions the strict applicability of the typology that had been recognised three years earlier (cf., Fig. 2.2, and Berry, 1963). In the 1966 study of Chicago the retail nucleations were first identified as areal units on the basis of land values. For the set of nucleations so identified the relationship between number of businesses and number of business types were examined using the then popular scattergram approach. The resultant distribution did not reveal the clear-cut groupings that the theory of tertiary activity postulates. Nevertheless, using that theory

Table 2.4 Provision of n commodities by a hierarchy of business centres within American cities (after Berry, *Commercial Structure and Commercial Blight*, 1963).

Type of centre	Commodities					
	$n, \ldots n-(i-1), n-i, \ldots n-(j-1), n-j, \ldots n-(k-1), n-k, \ldots, n-(m-1), n-m, \ldots, n-(p-1), n-p, \ldots, 2, 1$					
CBD	*	*	*	*	*	*
Regional		*	*	*	*	*
Other shopping			*	*	*	*
Community				*	*	*
Neighbourhood					*	*
Convenience						*

as a framework for his study Garner was forced to distinguish between the nucleations found in the areas of 'workingmen' and the 'rest' of the city. Examination of Garner's work shows this to be a reasonable decision dictated not by theory, which it contravenes, but by the empirical facts. The implication is therefore important, viz., the nature of the intra-urban central place system is effected and affected by the spatial variations in the socio-economic status and density distributions of the population.

It was found in Garner's study of Chicago that certain types of businesses varied in their presence and absence at different levels of the hierarchy. This accounts for part of the difficulties experienced by Garner in recognising the postulated hierarchy of tertiary nucleations. The conclusion was reached that it was inadvisable to rank business types on the basis of threshold values. The Chicago study showed that certain categories of business obviously had varying thresholds and ranges. This in turn prompted the equally important finding that the same category of business might in fact be operating at different levels on a quality scale in different parts of the city. The failure to recognise this fact at an earlier stage is probably attributable to the use of business directories for obtaining data. Thus two main findings of the 1966 study are that differences in the quality of businesses should be recognised, and provision should be made to allow for the fact that there appears to be a range of thresholds for each business type (Garner, 1966, pp. 115–18).

The commercial structure and hierarchy of nucleated shopping centres as recognised in Berry's typology is obviously based only on North American observation and experience. Even so the typology has been widely accepted as a framework for intra-urban research in other parts of the world without necessarily establishing its validity in such a situation. Indeed, even before its formal presentation, a study of the intra-urban system of central places in Zurich (Carol, 1960) concluded that an intra-urban hierarchy existed in that city. This conclusion was reached on the basis of field surveys that distinguished the kind and variety of commodities and services found at different levels of the city, backed up with sample data on their drawing power. It should be noted that the style of the Zurich study was less quantitatively oriented than those conducted in North America. Consequently its results though supporting the later theory of tertiary activity might have supported an alternative urban theory that postulated a hierarchy but not of the stepped kind.

Outside North America, however, a number of important differences between the form of tertiary nucleations and those incorporated in the theory of tertiary activity have been noted. It has, for example, been pointed out that the distinction between nucleated centres, urban arterial businesses and *beads* is not necessarily meaningful; particularly as *beads* and *arterials* along business thoroughfares in America were identified on intuitive notions (Clark, W. A. V., 1967, p. 24). Extra-CBD shopping areas in New Zealand have been found to have linear rather than nucleated form (Pownall, 1955; Clark, W. A. V., 1967) and this also appears to be the case in South Africa (Beavon, 1970a, 1972). In both instances clusters of shops have been termed shopping centres, corresponding to the American term *nucleated centre*, and it has not been found necessary to distinguish urban arterial business and automobile rows as distinctly different components of the commercial structure of cities. A similar conclusion has been drawn, on the basis of empirical work, on the way in which the businesses along the McCleod Trail in Calgary operate (Boal and Johnson, 1965). Notwithstanding these differences, intra-urban hierarchies of the type postulated by the theory of tertiary activity have been recognised in

Australia (Johnston, 1966) and New Zealand (Clark, W. A. V., 1967). However, the existence of structural continua of shopping centres have also been acknowledged in Australia (Johnston and Rimmer, 1967b; Walmsley, 1974).

It is appropriate at this point in the discussion to comment briefly on Johnston's (1966) study of the intra-metropolitan system of shopping centres in Melbourne. This study distinguishes an eight level hierarchy on the basis of numbers of business types and number of businesses recorded for 718 shopping centres. Johnston, like Garner (1966), makes use of data available from secondary sources (i.e., commercial directories) and this may have obscured certain variations in quality of businesses.

In the Melbourne study the spatial distribution of the resultant hierarchy was examined. It was found that there was a marked variation in its structure in different parts of the city. Although this is not a variation that could be expected either from central place theory of the theory of tertiary activity, a similar finding was made by Garner (1966) at approximately the same point in time.

A search of the literature provides little evidence for the strong support that has been claimed for the theory of tertiary activity at the intra-urban level other than from studies conducted in American cities (Carter, 1972, p. 95). Thus although a certain amount of tacit support has been advanced for the hierarchy postulated at the theoretical level it appears that such support has not necessarily been well founded. The sectoral and associated socio-economic variations in the nature and spatial distribution of the hierarchies in Chicago and Melbourne does bring to mind Lösch's model. However, it is not appropriate at this stage to discuss whether such a model might have provided a more appropriate framework for the study of intra-metropolitan shopping centres.

Apart from the explicit structural aspects of the urban hierarchy, it has also been shown above that the theory of tertiary activity embraces implicit behavioural aspects of consumers in the urban system. In even greater contrast to the empirical studies of the structural elements those of behavioural patterns in tertiary systems, at both the inter- and intra-city scale, have cast doubts on the implications of the theory.

Behavioural patterns

Initial doubts about the orderliness of consumer behaviour, as implied in the theory of tertiary activity, were first raised in an empirical study of non-farm households in Iowa (Thomas *et al.*, 1962). Further critical examination of the behavioural implications of the theory of tertiary activity have followed (Johnston, 1966; Golledge *et al.*, 1966; Clark, W. A. V., 1967; Johnston and Rimmer, 1967a; Rushton, Golledge and Clark, W. A. V., 1967; Clark, W. A. V., 1968; Clark and Rushton, 1970). Whereas only four of the studies (Johnston, 1966; Clark, W. A. V., 1967, 1968; Clark and Rushton, 1970) are explicitly concerned with the intra-urban system of central places, the findings in general throw doubt on the validity of the *nearest centre hypothesis*. The general conclusion is that consumers do not as a rule patronise the nearest centre either offering a particular commodity or possessing a particular business type. It has been found (Clark, W. A. V., 1968) that consumers travel significantly greater distances for the same commodity to centres at different levels in the hierarchy. However, it has also been concluded (Clark, W. A. V., 1968) that the rejection of the nearest centre hypothesis does not necessarily mean that there is no order in spatial behaviour. This conclusion has led to the search for an alternative behavioural model (Clark and Rushton, 1970) based on the notion that a consumer, in making a choice between alternative shopping centres, trades the advantages of centre size against the disadvantages of the distance that must be travelled to a shopping centre. The similarity of this approach to that used in gravity and probability models (e.g., Reilly, 1931; Huff, 1962; Lakshmanan and Hansen, 1965; see also the general discussion in Olsson, 1965) is apparent. In general the new approach makes use of indifference surfaces as the basis of the behavioural model.

The use of indifference maps as descriptions of individual preferences and attendant behaviour appears to have been introduced to geography by Edwards in 1954. The approach has been used in several studies concerned with behaviour in urban systems (Rushton *et al.*, 1967; Clark and Rushton, 1970; Rushton, 1969a, b, c, 1971). Recently a revision of central place theory has been attempted (Rushton, 1971) on the basis of behavioural patterns using space preference functions. This behavioural approach yielded a system of central places that differed in one important respect from the classic system of Christaller, and by implication, from the theory of tertiary activity; the activities in the centres occurred in *batches* that differed in composition for centres at the same level of the hierarchy. In consequence it was suggested that the concept of a *class* of centres belonging to a *level* in the step-like ranks of the hierarchy be abandoned. However, no associated attempt was made to revise the structural component of the theory of tertiary activity[6].

Attention has been directed to the effect of socio-economic variations on both the behavioural patterns of consumers and on the composition of businesses within shopping centres (R. L. Davies, 1968, 1969). In response it has been suggested (Beavon, 1970b) that physical and functional blight (as defined by Berry, 1963) in shopping centres might be regarded as surrogates of the attractiveness of shopping centres. This is also in accordance with the ideas expressed by Garner (1966). The deleterious effects of these blight forms on the attractive power of central places *vis-à-vis* less blighted central places, and their effect on the overall nature of a shopping centre, should be recognised and taken into account.

In the preceding discussion the reader will have noticed the interesting dichotomy that has reigned for some time in the field of central place studies. Namely the observation that a continuum is present in the data but the conclusion that a hierarchy exists. This is due in part to the techniques adopted for the recognition of a hierarchy and partly to the spirit of the times when much of the research was conducted. This point will be referred to again in Chapter 4.

In reviewing the literature devolving on the theory of tertiary activity and the internal composition of shopping centres within cities, the attention of the reader has been drawn to the doubts that have been cast on the validity of the theory of tertiary activity. It appears that a stepped hierarchy need not necessarily emerge in a metropolitan region in which the population and purchasing power is unevenly distributed. This in itself does not provide sufficient justification for discarding the theory of tertiary activity.

Notwithstanding these findings it appears desirable to re-examine the work of Christaller in detail. This is necessary for two major reasons. Firstly, the Christaller system of central places developed according to the marketing principle is based on the outer range of a commodity in contrast to the inner range or threshold employed in the theory of tertiary activity. Secondly, no full discussion of the derivation or of the interpretations that can be placed on Christaller's theory are evident in the literature.

Notes

1. As also evidenced by their continued reprinting in other publications (e.g. 1958a in Mayer and Kohn, 1959, and in Ambrose, 1969; 1958c in Leahy, McKee and Dean, 1970), and the continual reference to them in general texts on urban geography to date.
2. The threshold populations calculated in this way can only be *apparent* thresholds because all firms must be assumed to be earning only normal profits. The possibility that some firms may be earning excess or even sub-normal profits is either excluded or not recognised. (For similar comments see Robinson, 1968; Carter, 1972, p. 95.)
3. Published originally as *Die räumliche Ordnung der Wirtschaft; eine Untersuchung über Standort, Wirtschaftsgebiete und internationalen Handel* (1943), Fischer, Jena. All references to Lösch hereafter will be to the second revised edition translated by W. H. Woglom with the assistance of W. F. Stolper and published as *The Economics of Location* (1954), Yale University Press, New Haven.
4. In this book the term *commodity* is a substitute for the term *good* as used in much of the American literature on central place studies. However, there appears to be no reason why the term *business type* as also used in this study should not be freely substituted for *commodity*. This opinion has also been voiced by W. Davies (1967, pp. 78–9).
5. An earlier attempt (Marshall, 1964) to indicate certain discrepancies between the theory of tertiary activity and reality with a view to revising the theory has been completely rebuffed (by Berry, 1964). The rebuttal is based upon two supposed statements from the earlier paper by Berry and Garrison (1958c), but neither of the statements appear in that paper. (This observation has also been made by Saey, 1973.) Certainly the suggestions by Marshall for a revision of the theory of tertiary activity appear sound but were not followed up by him. It seems as though Marshall accepted the criticism of Berry, as his own later work (Marshall, 1969) is based on the theory of tertiary activity in an unmodified form.
6. Mitchell *et al.*, (1974) have recently attempted to expand on the work of Rushton (1971).

Chapter 3

Christaller re-examined

A review of the early literature concerned with the location and size of settlements has shown that Machiavelli (1531) can be regarded as one of the earliest central place theorists (Dawson, 1969). However, it was Lalanne (1863), working at the interface of mathematics and geography, who was among the first to introduce the concept of a homogeneous plane with an even distribution of population. Furthermore Lalanne was able to show how a hexagonal system of town sites would emerge on such a surface. Notwithstanding, it fell to Walter Christaller in 1933 to draw upon the work of Kohl (1850) and Gradmann (1916) and to synthesise the ideas then existing on the nature of the location of urban places, and in so doing to make his distinguished and original contribution to the field of central place studies[1]. *Die zentralen Orte in Süddeutschland* by Christaller is now recognised as the seminal work in the field of central place studies notwithstanding the similar work of less well known American rural sociologists[2] (Galpin, 1915; Kolb, 1923; Kolb and Polson, 1933; Kolb and Brunner, 1946).

Towards a system of central places

Recognising that a satisfactory distinction had been made between rural and urban settlements by Gradmann in 1926, Christaller set out to explain the observed variation in the size and spacing of towns that performed the role of central places[3]. In so doing Christaller clearly manifested his firm belief that some ordering principle governed the distribution of central places. As a prologue to the development of his central place model Christaller introduced a descriptive terminology of the elements to be used. The region served by a central place was termed its *complementary region*. Central places whose *central activities*[4] extended their influence over a large area were termed *central places of high order*, whereas central places whose activities were less extensive in influence were described as *central places of lower order*. The service limit of each central activity was described by the *outer limit of the range of the commodity* in which it dealt.

Christaller took pains to make it clear that the demand for and the consumption of central commodities would depend *inter alia* upon the distribution of and socio-economic variations in the population, and upon the degree to which the population was concentrated in any particular central place. Demand for central activities would also be dependent upon the distance, including effort distance, that persons had to travel to obtain the commodities. It was assumed that demand would fall off to zero with increasing distance from the central place (Christaller, 1966, pp. 27—47).

Thus it is clear from the early parts of his study that Christaller was aware that the vagaries of space create uneven patterns for the demand and consumption of central commodities. However, he did not constrain his theoretical model of settlement by assuming it to be developed on an isotropic surface, i.e., a homogeneous plane surface with an even distribution of population. Several general texts, notably by Bunge (1962, p. 130), Alexander (1963, pp. 560—1), Thoman *et al.* (1968, pp. 205—7), Abler *et al.* (1971, pp. 370—2), Yeates and Garner (1971, pp. 200—3), Haggett (1972, pp. 285—9), Hurst (1972, pp. 198—203), Lloyd and Dicken (1972, pp. 14—15), have given the impression that Christaller explicitly assumed an isotropic surface. Nowhere did Christaller specify an isotropic surface[5]. Another common interpretation of Christaller's work is that he developed his central place systems on the basis of the minimum conditions required for a commodity to be offered in a market system[6]. This assumption has been made in work by Berry (1967, pp. 64—5), Marshall (1969, pp. 16—18) and Lloyd and Dicken (1972, pp. 14—15).

With these comments in mind, the concept of the range of a commodity as used by Christaller will be re-examined, from which it will become clear that it is correct to infer that he merely assumed a uniform transportation surface on which to develop his theoretical model.

The concept of the range

In any discussion of the *range of central commodities* it must be emphasised that the term represented the simultaneous spatial effects of many factors. These included demand (indicated by the size of the population), income distribution, transportation facilities and other market conditions which work interdependently to establish the range of any central commodity or service (Christaller, 1966, p. 49). The range, therefore, was not only the maximum distance the dispersed population would be willing to travel to purchase a particular commodity offered at a central place, but also, because the economic nature of distance was emphasised, the range was specific to particular persons. Consequently, every commodity had its own special range. The same commodity had a different range at each central place and its range would not be equal in all directions about any one central place (Christaller, 1966, p. 53). Furthermore, 'the range is not shaped like a circle, but rather varies according to the objective economic distance and the subjective economic distance, i.e., it is irregularly shaped like a star' (Christaller, 1966, p.´54). This statement is apparently contradicted within the same argument by Christaller, for he goes on to state (1966, p. 54) that the range manifests itself spatially as a ring viz.,

When we examine this range in detail, we find, in looking at it spatially, that there is not a line, but rather a ring around the central place. It has an outer (or upper) and an inner (or lower) limit. The upper limit of a particular good [commodity] is determined by the farthest distance from the central place from which it can be obtained from this central place; and indeed, beyond this limit it will either not be obtained, or it will be obtained from another central place. In the first case, the absolute limit (ideal range) is reached; and in the latter case the relative limit (real range) is reached. Up to the present, we have called however inexactly, this upper limit of the range simply the range.

The ambiguity is apparent if on the one hand a *ring* is taken to be annular in form as opposed to an undulating rim (an interpretation apparently taken by Getis and Getis, 1966, p. 221; and Carter, 1972, p. 73). On the other hand, it is possible that the first phrase of the above paragraph should read: 'When we examine the range under the conditions of a uniform transportation surface . . .' Only thus can the ambiguity between the statements that the shape of the range is irregular and star-like and that it is circular be resolved. It is concluded that a transportation surface must have been assumed, for only then can the apparent gap between Christaller's consideration of real world situations and the presentation of his deduced system of central places (Christaller, 1966, p. 60 *et seq.*) be bridged. The use of circular limits to the range of commodities as presented in Fig. 3.1 and statements that different order places have different population sizes (Christaller, 1966, pp. 59–60, 66–8) are then reconciled.

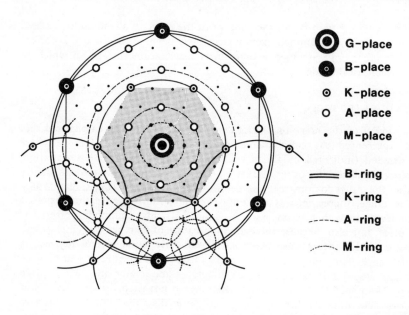

Fig. 3.1   The emergence of a system of central places according to the marketing principle. Christaller's dashed circle shown about the G-place appears to serve no positive purpose (after Christaller, *Central Places in Southern Germany*, 1966, p. 61).

On the assumption that a uniform transportation surface was originally envisaged by Christaller, the relationships between the different ranges can be examined diagrammatically, with the radii for the lower and the upper limits of the range set as L_r and U_r respectively (Fig. 3.2). When the same commodity can be obtained from another central place, a *real range* becomes apparent. The lower limit of the range is determined by the minimum amount of demand for this central commodity needed to pay for the production or offering of the commodity (Christaller, 1966, p. 54). If a neighbouring central place offers the same commodity (C), and if that place is located at a distance d from the first central place, then the *real range* of the commodity is reduced to $d/2$ along a line between the

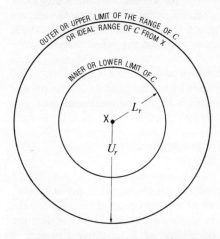

Fig. 3.2   Relationship between the inner and outer limits of the range of a commodity *C* offered from X (from Beavon, *Environmental Studies*, **15**, 1975).

two places, and will be offered from both places provided

$$L_r \leqslant d/2 \tag{3.1}$$

This situation is shown in Fig. 3.3.

Having stated that various factors affect the inner and outer limits of the range of a commodity, the exact ratio between the two limits could not be expressed by Christaller. However, it is clear that where the value of L_r is small the possibility of the commodity in question being offered from other central places is increased (cf., Christaller, 1966, p. 56). Thus as the lower limit of a commodity increased in value the possibility of it being offered from neighbouring central places decreased. If the lower limit of a commodity exceeded the upper limit then the central commodity

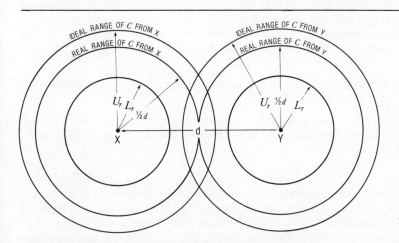

Fig. 3.3   Relationship between the ideal and the real range of a commodity *C* offered from X and Y (from Beavon, op. cit., **15**, 1975).

would not be offered at all. If the actual patronage for the central commodity came only from within the zone bounded by the inner limit of the range then the income would just cover expenditures, and there would be no profits (Christaller, 1966, p. 55). The rings created by the inner and outer limits of the range therefore constituted the spatial projection of the net profits of the owner of the central business, which equalled the difference between sales and costs (Christaller, 1966, p. 55). Thus the ring bounded by the inner limit of the range of a commodity was described as analogous to the economic domain of the conventional cost and revenue curves (Baskin, 1966, fn. in Christaller, 1966, p. 55).

The system of central places

Christaller's original presentation of the system of central places employed specific arithmetic measures of distance for the ranges of central commodities and for the distances between central places in the system. As Carter (1972) points out, the introduction of exact measures in the development of a deductive structure is regrettable. Although justification for the measures is provided the critical and exact values of 36, 21, 12 and 7 km suggested by Christaller to separate successively lower order central places from one another is initially confusing. The system of central places, as first presented, consisted of five orders of central places, designated as G-, B-, K-, A- and M-places [7]. Commencing with the distribution of a particular commodity with an outer limit of the range of 21 km from an isolated B-place (G in Fig. 3.1), Christaller showed that it was not possible to provide a commodity with an outer limit of the range of 20 km from that B-place to the area lying between 20 and 21 km from it. On the assumption that the commodity with a range of 20 km should be supplied to all areas, the introduction of additional central places became necessary to accomplish the task. Similarly, it was shown that only by the introduction of K-, A- and M-places would it be possible to provide all commodities with an outer limit of the range of less than 21 km to the area enclosed by the 36 km ring, on which the additional B-places were located (Fig. 3.1) (Christaller, 1966, pp. 61–2). Thereafter the initial B-place found itself central to six B-places and was upgraded to a G-place. Having briefly outlined the nature of the central place system a general derivation can now be presented. This derivation will also be based upon the outer limit of the range of particular commodities.

A general derivation of central places according to the marketing principle

In presenting a general derivation of the system of central places, the derivation will proceed down the hierarchy from an initial B-place as was the case in Christaller's original work.

B-places

In developing a system of central places to serve a region Christaller's objective was to create a system that provided maximum coverage from a minimum number of supply points (Christaller, 1966, p. 63). It follows therefore that whatever order of central place is first introduced must be arranged in an equilateral lattice pattern. This ensures that the central places are equidistant from their nearest neighbours, with a minimum of overlap between their circular supply areas as demarcated by the outer limit of the range of their highest order commodity. Thus the distance between the B-places, the order of central place selected by Christaller as the commencing point in his central place development, must be a function of the radius of the supply area of their highest order commodity C_n. Let the outer limit of the range of the commodity C_n be k units (where n is a relatively large integer), and let the lower limit of its range be such that it is distributed from a central place B' (i.e., at the location of what will become the G-place in Fig. 3.1).

For the purpose of discussion consider a set of seven B-places (Figs 3.4 and 3.5). The six central places around the one at their centre, designated B', can be designated $B_1, B_2, \ldots B_6$. Each of these *seven* B-places will now supply commodity C_n to an outer limit of k units. As it is the object of the B central places, equidistant from each other, to supply commodity C_n to all parts of the region within k

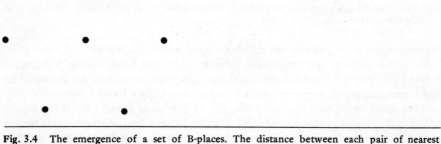

Fig. 3.4 The emergence of a set of B-places. The distance between each pair of nearest neighbouring B-places is a function of the radius of the outer range of its highest order commodity.

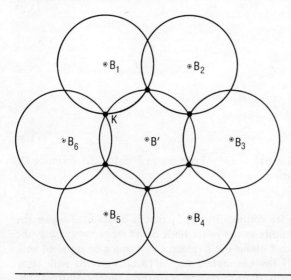

Fig. 3.5 Six equidistant B-places arranged about B'. K-places will emerge at the intersection of each set of three radial limits of k units drawn about B' and the B-places (from Beavon, op. cit., 15, 1975).

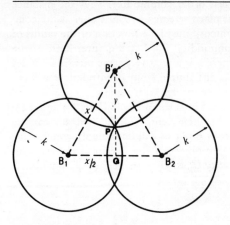

Fig. 3.6   The distance relationship between any two nearest neighbour B-places and the central B'-place (from Beavon, op. cit., **15**, 1975).

units of them, it follows that the circular supply areas must overlap each other (Fig. 3.5). As all B-places are equidistant from their nearest neighbouring B-places, it follows that a set of three nearest neighbouring B-places constitute the apexes of an equilateral triangle. The intersection of the exclusive supply limits from such supply centres must be at the median point (P) of a triangle formed by three supply centres, B', B_1, B_2, for example (Fig. 3.6). It follows from elementary geometry that B'Q is perpendicular to B_1B_2 and that B'Q is 1.5 times the length of B'P. Let the distance B'B_1, B_1Q and B'P of the triangle B'B_1Q in Fig. 3.6 be designated x, $x/2$ and y respectively. Then

$$x^2 = x^2/4 + 9y^2/4 \tag{3.2}$$

Therefore

$$3x^2/4 = 9y^2/4$$

and

$$x^2 = 3y^2$$

whence

$$x = y\sqrt{3} \tag{3.3}$$

As the distance y in Fig. 3.6 has already been set to k units, the distance D_B between any two B-places is given as

$$D_B = k\sqrt{3} \tag{3.4}$$

Consider the next lower order commodity C_{n-1} that is distributed under the same conditions but has $k - d$ units as the outer limit of its range; where d is the width of a ring, within the radius k about the B'-place, that cannot be supplied with commodity C_{n-1} (Fig. 3.7). If the unsupplied ring is to be supplied with commodity C_{n-1} then it will be necessary to provide *at least three* supply centres offering such a commodity[8]. Such supply centres will necessarily be equidistant from each other and will overlap one another (Fig. 3.8). An alternative solution that both

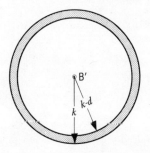

Fig. 3.7   Unsupplied area about B′ (shaded). A commodity with $k - d$ units as its outer limit of the range cannot be supplied from B′ to the shaded area (from Beavon, op. cit., 15, 1975).

minimises the overlap and that recognises the prior existence of the set of B-places is possible. This solution will lead to the emergence of a lower order central place termed a K-place.

K-places
Let the successive differences between the outer limits of the ranges of successively lower order commodities be d_i ($i = 1, 2, 3, \ldots$). It follows that any commodity supplied from a B-place that has an outer limit of the range less than k units cannot be supplied to all parts of the area within a circle of radius $k\sqrt{3}$ about B′ (Fig. 3.9). Christaller's requirement that all areas must be supplied with all commodities necessitates the introduction of other central places called K-places, located at those points furthest from but between their neighbouring B-places, i.e., the median points. Here the K-places provide the unsupplied parts of the region around the B-places with the commodities that have an outer limit of the range [9] equal to or less than $k - d_1$ i.e., commodities of order less than or equal to C_{n-1}. The B-places

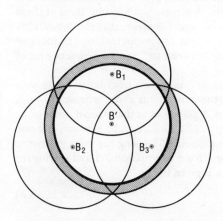

Fig. 3.8   The complete supply of the unsupplied ring about B′ (also shown in Fig. 3.7) *can be* achieved by providing three additional supply centres each distributing to a distance $k - d$ units (from Beavon, op. cit., 15, 1975).

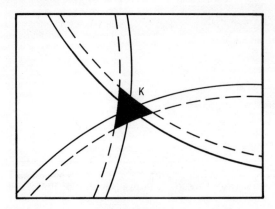

Fig. 3.9 The emergence of K-places. Unsupplied areas (shaded) emerge as the outer limit of the range of the commodities supplied from B-places becomes less than k units (indicated by solid lines), e.g., becomes $k - d_1$ units (indicated by dashed lines). K-places will emerge to supply the unsupplied area (from Beavon, op. cit., **15**, 1975).

will also supply all commodities with an outer limit of the range less than k. In this case the distance D_K between any two K-places is given as

$$D_K = k \qquad (3.5)$$

A-places

A commodity C_{n-j} that is supplied from any nearest neighbour set of two K-places and a B-place to an outer limit of $k - d_j$ units will only just be provided to all parts of the region between these places. Thus any commodity $C_{n-(j+\alpha)}$ (where α is a positive integer), with an outer limit of the range of $k - d_{j+\alpha}$ units, supplied by two K-places and a B-place will not be supplied to all parts of the region between them. It is only by introducing other central places, A-places, and locating them at those points furthest from but between two K-places and a B-place, that the commodity $C_{n-(j+\alpha)}$ can be supplied to all parts of the region under discussion. The location of A-places will be at the median points lying between any nearest neighbour set of two K-places and a B-place (cf. Fig. 3.1).

The distance between a place of any order and its nearest neighbours of equal or higher order can be calculated in the same manner as set out above when calculating the distance between two B-places. Thus, an A-place lies at the median point of an equilateral triangle of side k (the distance between a B-place and a K-place, and also the distance between any two K-places; cf. equation 3.5). Using the same geometric relationships as given in Fig. 3.6, substituting k for x in equation 3.3 and solving for y, the distance D_A between any two A-places, is given by

$$D_A = k/\sqrt{3} \qquad (3.6)$$

M-places

The derivation and location of the M-places follows the same procedure. The occurrence of M-places becomes necessary when the supply of commodity C_{n-l} with an outer limit range of $k - d_l$ units $(l > j)$ from the existing central places, is just capable of reaching all parts of the region. The supply of $C_{n-(1+\alpha)}$ to an outer limit of $k - d_{1+\alpha}$ is only possible if M-places are introduced and located at the median points between two nearest neighbour A-places and their nearest K- or B-place. The M-places will provide all commodities with an outer limit of the range less than $k - d_l$, as will all other existing central places. The distance between M- and A-places is calculated as before with the distance $k/\sqrt{3}$ from equation 3.6 being substituted for x in equation 3.3, and again solving for y. The distance D_M between any two neighbouring M-places or between any M-place and nearest neighbouring higher order place is therefore given as

$$D_M = k/3 \tag{3.7}$$

H-places

Christaller did consider the possibility of introducing H-places, an order of central places below the M-places, but rejected these since he felt that H-places would not be characteristic central places in that they would have no central importance and could exercise few central roles (Christaller, 1966, p. 62).

Range of the region of a central place

The circular boundaries around central places of different orders (i.e., the B-, K-, A- and M-rings of Fig. 3.1) represent the outer limit of the range of the lowest order *commodity* that can be offered from the central place before it becomes necessary to introduce another lower level of central places to ensure that *all* commodities are available to all areas in the system. It is this particular range that Christaller has termed the *range of region.*.

It should be clear from the discussion above, and from Fig. 3.1, that the *range of region* of each order of central place is equal to the distance between itself and its nearest neighbour of immediate lower order. As the distance between any two nearest neighbouring central places of the same order is $1/\sqrt{3}$ of the distance between two nearest neighbouring central places of immediately higher order, it follows that the range of region of central places of successively lower order will be $1/\sqrt{3}$ of the range of region for the previously higher order. Thus

$$R_j = D_j/\sqrt{3} \tag{3.8}$$

where R_j is the range of a region j, j is a particular order of central place and D_j is the distance between two nearest neighbouring central places of order j. These relationships are shown in Table 3.1.

Table 3.1 Relationships between nearest neighbour distances and the *range of region* for central places of the B-system according to the marketing principle (from Beavon, op. cit., 15, 1975).

Order of central place	Distance between nearest neighbours of the same order	Range of region
B	$k\sqrt{3}$	k
K	k	$k/\sqrt{3}$
A	$k/\sqrt{3}$	$k/3$
M	$k/3$	$k/3\sqrt{3}$

Completing the hierarchy

Central commodities with an outer limit of the range greater than k units can only be offered from the B′-place if the lower limit of the range is such that these commodities can only be offered from one place in the region (Christaller, 1966, p. 63). Thus the first B-place (B′ in this discussion cf., Fig. 3.5) becomes a higher order G-place. From the nature of the deductive structure of the central place system discussed so far it should be clear that a G-place will have a range of region of $k\sqrt{3}$. For a seven-level hierarchy two higher order places need to be introduced, the P-place and the L-place. The P- and L-places have ranges of region equal to $3k$ and $3k\sqrt{3}$ respectively [10].

Following the selection of 4 km as *the* range of region for an M-place[11] (Christaller, 1966, p. 62) all the general distances derived above can be converted to the actual distances adopted by Christaller (Table 3.2).

Table 3.2   Distances in kilometers computed from a given distance of 4 km as the *range of region* for M-places and the derived relationship that distances increase by $\sqrt{3}$ up the hierarchy. Distances used by Christaller in his initial description are given in parentheses (from Beavon, op. cit., **15**, 1975).

Type of central place and order		Distance between nearest neighbours of same order (km)		Range of region (km)	
L	7th	—	—	108.0	(108)
P	6th	108.0	(108)	62.4	(62)
G	5th	62.4	(62)	36.0	(36)
B	4th	36.0	(36)	20.8	(21)
K	3rd	20.8	(21)	12.0	(12)
A	2nd	12.0	(12)	6.9	(7)
M	1st	6.9	(7)	4.0	(4)

The emergence of hexagonal marketing regions

Christaller having derived the central place system, albeit using exact values for the ranges of commodities, the complementary regions, shown as overlapping circles in Fig. 3.1, could be depicted schematically as regular hexagons (Christaller, 1966, p. 66). The schematic representation is reproduced here as Fig. 3.10, and further illustrated by Fig. 3.11. Christaller did not specifically explain why the overlapping circular market areas should be treated as non-overlapping hexagons. However, the creation of the hexagons, achieved through the simple division of the overlapping portions of the circular market regions, was in accordance with the concept of the real range (Christaller, 1966, p. 57), viz.,

the ideal range reaches to the full limit of the range of the central good from an isolated central place, whereas the real range reaches to where the central good can be obtained with greater advantage from a neighbouring central place. Segments are everywhere cut away from the ideal circle-forming complementary regions of the isolated central place, and these segments belong to the complimentary regions of the neighbouring central places.

Furthermore it was pointed out that 'The areas of the hexagonal market regions are equal to the area of the circle minus six segments.' (Christaller, 1966, p. 66.) Thus

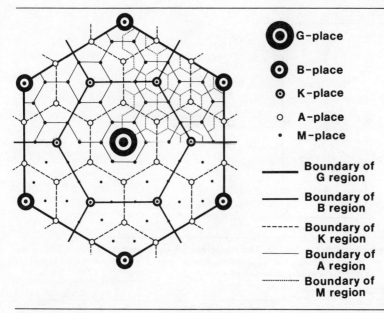

G-place
B-place
K-place
A-place
M-place

———— Boundary of
      G region

———— Boundary of
      B region

------- Boundary of
      K region

———— Boundary of
      A region

·············· Boundary of
      M region

Fig. 3.10 Schematic representation of the market regions of the system of central places developed according to the marketing principle (after Christaller, *Central Places in Southern Germany*, 1966, p. 66).

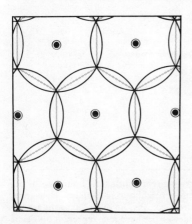

Fig. 3.11 The emergence of the hexagonal B-region. The overlap between the circular supply regions of commodity C_n to a radius k units about the B-places is formally divided by straight indifference lines.

the introduction of hexagons by Christaller appears more positive than a mere tidying up of the diagram of overlapping circular regions as suggested by Marshall (1969, pp. 18–19).

For the sake of clarity it appears desirable at this stage to summarise the foregoing discussion and to do so in a graphic manner. For this reason the emergence of

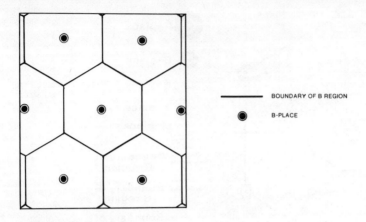

Fig. 3.12   A B-region about a B-place. The emergence of the lower order places within the B-region is shown in the following set of diagrams. For comparative purposes the development of the surrounding B-regions will be shown feintly.

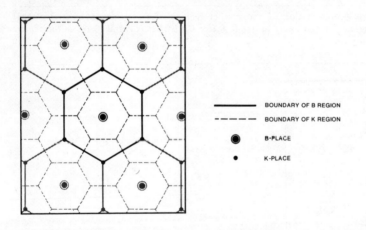

Fig. 3.13   The K-places emerge at the points of the hexagon representing the boundary of the B-region. The K-places are *k* units away from their nearest neighbouring B-places. Hexagonal supply areas emerge about the K-places and demarcate the K-regions. As these hexagons are the boundaries of the effective range of the K-places, the sides of the hexagons represent points of indifference between adjacent central places. The boundaries of the hexagons are drawn at right angles to the imaginary lines linking two nearest neighbouring K-places, or K- and B-places.

the central places in a B-region (and adjacent B-regions) is shown by a set of diagrams (Figs 3.12 to 3.15).

Having developed a system of central places according to the marketing principle, Christaller considered two other systems: the first a system derived according to a transportation principle; secondly, one derived according to an administrative principle[12]. In each system the initial ordering of the hierarchy of central places was determined by one of these governing principles and, thereafter,

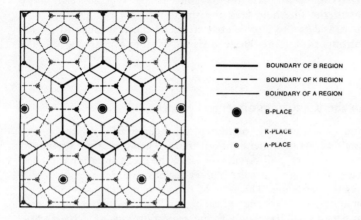

Fig. 3.14 The emergence of the A-places at the points on the hexagons representing the boundary of the K-regions. The A-places lie at the median points between sets of nearest neighbouring K- and B-places.

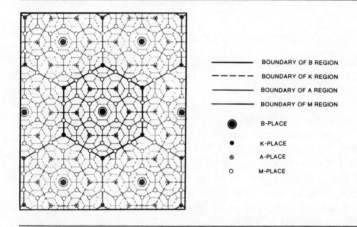

Fig. 3.15 The emergence of the M-places at points on the hexagons representing the boundary of the A-regions. The M-places lie at the median points between sets of nearest neighbouring A-places and K-places, or B-places.

a market system was superimposed using the principles developed in the initial model. Although attempts were later made to integrate the three models into a single model (Christaller, 1950 and 1960) the success of the operation is dubious. It is the system of central places based on the marketing principle, dubbed by Lösch (1954, p. 130) as the $k = 3$ system, and now generally known as the K3 system, that continues to characterise the central place theory of Christaller and from which the theory of tertiary activity (Berry and Garrison, 1958c) has evolved. For this reason the discussion that follows will be concerned only with the central place system developed according to the marketing principle. To date the interpretation of this system of central places appears to have been superficial at best and in some cases incorrect. The discussion that follows concentrates on the relationship between the extent of the threshold area and the outer limit of the range of a commodity, it also considers the inter-related effect of the real range of a commodity that is introduced by the linear division of the overlapping circular marketing regions.

Profit domains in the K3 system of central places

The system of central places is clearly predicated on the basis of the outer limit of the range of a commodity. As the inner limit or threshold can vary, the existence of profits and the amount of such profits will also vary. The profit situation is further complicated when the overlapping circular market regions (Fig. 3.1) are schematically presented as regular hexagons. The sides of the hexagons represent the equal division of the overlapping circular range of the region. Tacit in this arrangement is the assumption that persons will travel only to the nearest offering of a commodity. It is necessary to remember that the range of the region does *not* correspond with the outer limit of the range of the highest order commodity offered by the central place of that region. The consequent effect of the hexagonal boundaries on profits are thus not readily apparent and require closer examination. As a preliminary step the relationship between two places of successive order will first be considered.

Relationship between B-places and K-places

For purposes of illustration consider only the K- and B-places of the K3 system presented in Figs 3.1 and 3.10. Whereas the effects of varying thresholds on profits can be illustrated by considering only the relationship between a single K- and B-place (Fig. 3.16), the actual situation is more complex. This is so since each K-place has as nearest higher order neighbours two B-places and a G-place, and as nearest neighbours of the same order three K-places, with six A-places as nearest neighbours of immediately lower order (Fig. 3.10).

From the general distance relationships already derived (Table 3.2), the distance between a K-place and a B-place is k units. As already shown, the B-place can supply a commodity C_n with an outer limit of the range of k units (this corresponds to the actual case of commodity Number 21 and an outer limit of the range of 21 km as used in the original text by Christaller, 1966, p. 60). In addition a B-place

Fig. 3.16 Relationships between B-places and K-places (cf., Figs 3.1, 3.10 and 3.11). The ▶ distance between the K- and B-places is set at k units. The boundary of indifference (heavy dots) is $k/2$ between K and B. The outer limits of the range of commodities C_{n+1}, C_n, and C_{n-1} to C_{n-11} are shown by bars in the upper and lower parts of the diagram (a and c respectively), and as radial curves about K and B in the central part (b). Commodity C_{n-9} determines the range of region (heavy lines in part b). If k is set to 21 km, to correspond with the value set by Christaller, then the figures on the left indicate the outer limit of the range in kilometres for successively lower order commodities, where the difference is expressed according to equation 3.9 (in the text). The circles about A (in part b) indicate the outer limits of the range of commodity C_{n-10} (11 km) and lower order commodities offered from the A-place.

The middle part of the diagram represents a part of Fig. 3.1; the upper part is a cross-section between K and B of the middle part, excluding the A-place; the lower part *represents* a cross-section between K and A of the middle part. It is important to note that the distance K to A is greater than $k/2$ units and the cross-section in (c) has been adjusted to accommodate this (from Beavon, op. cit., 15, 1975).

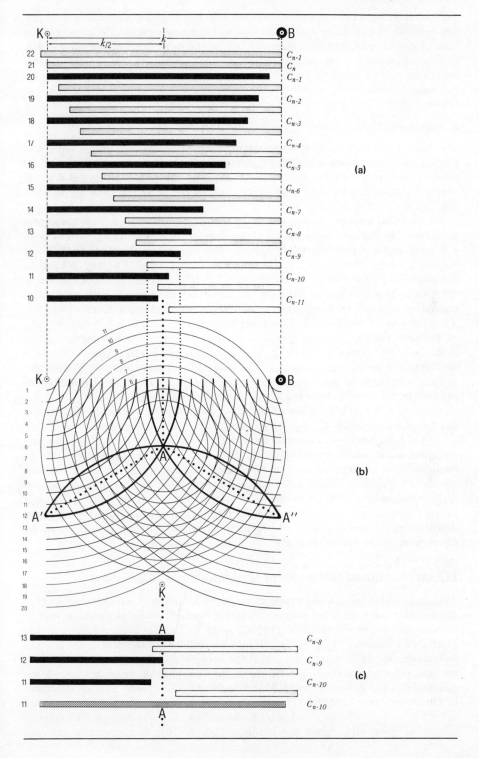

may offer commodities with an outer limit of the range in excess of k units, but *will* offer all commodities with outer limits of the range less than k units. For the sake of convenience let the difference between the outer limit of the range of any pair of successively lower order commodities be d_0. It follows that the next highest order commodity below C_n will be C_{n-1} with an outer limit of the range of $k - d_0$. Successively lower order commodities will be C_{n-i} with outer limit ranges of $k - d_i$ where

$$d_i = id_0 \ (i = 1, 2, 3, \ldots) \tag{3.9}$$

The highest order commodity supplied from a K-place will be C_{n-1}. This commodity will be supplied to a distance of $k - d_0$ units[13]. The commodity C_{n-1} is also supplied from B-places over the same distance. Likewise both K- and B-places supply all other commodities with outer limits of the range less than $k - d_0$ units (Fig. 3.16).

As the outer limit of the range of the commodities C_{n-i} decreases, so the extent of the overlap between market areas of the identical commodities supplied by both a K-place and a B-place decreases (Fig. 3.16a). The range of the region[14] of a K-place has been shown to be $k/\sqrt{3}$ (from equations 3.5 and 3.8), and is equal to the outer limit of the range of commodity C_{n-9} (Fig. 3.16a and c). The division of the overlapping portions of the circular market region with radius $k - 9d_0$ (i.e., equivalent to $k/\sqrt{3}$ in the general case) effectively introduces a division line (Fig. 3.16b) or *line of indifference* (Lloyd and Dicken, 1972, p. 12) that forms the sides of the resultant hexagonal market area. As it is clear from the statements already made (and in Christaller, 1966, p. 57), persons located only to the left of the indifference line in Fig. 3.16a will now obtain the commodities C_{n-i} from the K-place, and those to the right of the line will visit only the B-place. The effect of the indifference line is to make the *real range* of commodities $C_{n-1}, \ldots, C_{n-9}$ equal to each other[15]. Along a line between the K-place and the B-place this is also true for commodity C_{n-10}.

Profits have previously been represented as the difference between the inner and the outer limits of the range of a commodity. It is appropriate at this stage to introduce the concept of normal and excess profits. When the inner limit or *threshold* of a commodity exactly equals the outer limit of the range (or the real range) then, in accordance with the terminology used so far, no profits are earned but the firm is in a position to operate. Such a situation is more appropriately described as a *normal profits* situation. It follows that *excess profits* would be represented by the excess range available over the threshold requirements.

Effects of assumed relationships between threshold and range

The introduction of the real range, through the behavioural assumption that consumers minimise their travel distance, need not preclude excess profits being earned on the sale of the commodities[16] C_{n-1} to C_{n-9}. However, whatever excess profits were theoretically possible will now be reduced. In the case of the generalised illustration (Fig. 3.16a) the real range becomes $k/2$. In order to proceed any further, assumptions about the nature of the threshold requirements for all the commodities C_{n-i} must be made. This is necessary as there is no explicit statement in Christaller's text (1966) on the extent of the threshold for various commodities. Indeed it is clear that the thresholds of commodities can vary even to the extent of surpassing their ideal range (Christaller, 1966, p. 56). Five mutually exclusive assumptions appear to cover all the possibilities viz., the extent of the threshold

(a) is an absolute figure and remains constant for all commodities,
(b) increases proportionately with a decrease in the outer limit of the range of a commodity,
(c) is a constant proportion of the outer limit of the range of a commodity,
(d) is a variable proportion of the outer limit of the range of a commodity but varies in such a way that lower order commodities will have lower thresholds, or
(e) bears a random relationship with the outer limits of the range for any commodity.

The first three possibilities (a, b, c above) are naturally dependent on the *prior* assumption of an evenly distributed population. *For the purpose of argument let this be the case.*

Threshold as an absolute constant
If the extent of the threshold is fixed and is less than the real range of the highest order commodity in a central place system, then all commodities with an outer limit of the range exceeding the real range will earn the same amount of excess profit. This assumption also implies that, effectively, the threshold increases as a percentage of the outer limit of the range as the order of the commodity decreases. Such a specific case is considered next.

Threshold as an increasing proportion of range
If the extent of the threshold is initially set equal to the real range of the highest order commodity, and this relationship is maintained as the order of the commodity decreases, then only normal profits at best will be possible in all cases. This is an extreme assumption but has been implied in at least one recent text (i.e., Haggett, 1972, p. 288).

Threshold as a constant proportion of range
Suppose that the extent of the threshold is always a fixed percentage of the outer limit of the range of a commodity, then the threshold will decline constantly as the outer limit of the range or order of the commodity decreases (Fig. 3.17). Under these assumed circumstances excess profits will be possible on all the commodities C_{n-i} in the present example, provided that the extent of the threshold is less than 52.5 per cent of the outer limit of the range of a commodity [17]. However, if the threshold is 70 per cent of the outer limit of the range of a commodity then excess profits can only be earned for commodities C_{n-7} and lower order; normal profits will be earned in the case of commodity C_{n-6} and, on the assumption that normal profits are essential for a commodity to be offered at all, there will be no offering of commodities C_{n-1} to C_{n-5}. Regardless of the exact proportion assumed between the extent of the threshold and the outer limit of the range, the absolute amount of the excess profits will increase proportionately as the order of the commodity decreases. In general the relationship discussed here appears to be a popularly held assumption about thresholds and the outer limit of the range of a commodity (Berry and Garrison, 1958a, b, c; Abler *et al.*, 1971, p. 370; Yeates and Garner, 1971, p. 202; Hurst, 1972, p. 202; Lloyd and Dicken, 1972, p. 13).

The assumption that the extent of the threshold is a constant proportion of the range implies that certain commodities might be excluded from the market.

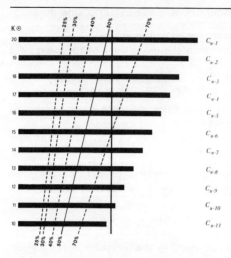

Fig. 3.17 Relationships between the outer limit of the range of a commodity C_α (solid bars) and assumed thresholds. The vertical line corresponds to the real range of $k/2$ units in Fig. 3.16. Dashed lines indicate threshold as a percentage of the outer limit of the range of different commodities. If threshold distance is less than 52.5 per cent of the outer limit of the range of a commodity for this example as discussed in the text, then excess profits will be earned (from Beavon, op. cit., 15, 1975).

Furthermore for this assumption to be considered tenable it is essential, as already indicated, that population be evenly distributed. Thus acceptance of the assumption that the extent of the threshold is a constant proportion of the outer limit of the range of a commodity leads to a conflict with Christaller's own statements. It appears clear that Christaller assumed not an isotropic plane, but a transportation plane with a regular but uneven distribution of population. The latter surface allows large populations to be found within a small radius about high order central places. Thus the radius of a *threshold area* is likely to be only a small percentage of the outer limit of the range in the case of high order central places, but a higher percentage in the case of lower order central places. On this basis the assumption that the extent of the threshold area is a constant proportion of the outer limit of the range must be rejected.

Threshold as a varying proportion of range
Assuming the extent of the threshold to be a varying proportion of the outer limit of the range of a commodity produces a situation similar to that just considered. Excess profits will appear at a particular rank in the order of commodities offered depending on what initial percentage of the outer limit of the range is assumed by the threshold, provided the ideal range is greater than the extent of the threshold. Thereafter, all lower order commodities will earn excess profits but the amount of such profits will not be constantly proportionate to the decline in the outer limit of their ranges (Fig. 3.18). It appears that this assumption has not previously been made about Christaller's work. Nevertheless, as different order places have different population sizes (Christaller, 1966, p. 60, pp. 66–7), threshold populations for any order of commodity are likely to be drawn from threshold areas of different size. Consequently the radius of the threshold area will not necessarily decrease in

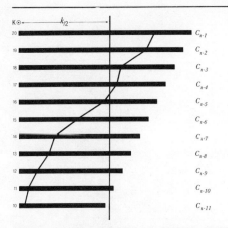

Fig. 3.18 Relationship between threshold as an irregular but decreasing proportion of the outer limit of the range of commodity C_α. If the vertical line at $k/2$ units from K is the real limit of the range, and the diagonally running line indicates the threshold limit for each commodity, then excess profits are only available for commodities of rank lower than C_{n-5} (from Beavon, op. cit., **15**, 1975).

constant proportion to the decrease in the outer limit of the range of the commodities. This assumption therefore appears attractive.

Threshold as a random proportion of range

If it is assumed that the threshold is a random proportion of the outer limit of the range of a commodity then there will be no recognisable relationship between the outer limit of the range of a commodity and its threshold requirements. In some cases excess profits, and in others only normal profits, will be earned, and still other commodities will not be offered at all. There will be no clear relationship between the amount of excess profits and the order of the commodity (Fig. 3.19).

In a real world situation there is little reason why either assumption (a) or (b) above should find favour. Similarly, there is little reason why (c) should be preferred to the exclusion of (d) and (e). From the point of view of theoretical modelling assumption (c), that the extent of the threshold is a constant proportion of the outer limit of the range of a commodity, is attractive and easy to work with. As cited above, it appears to enjoy popular support but conflicts with Christaller's assumption that population is not evenly distributed. The vagaries of the real business world are more closely represented by a situation best described as a combination of assumptions (d) and (e), namely, that thresholds for commodities tend to decrease as the outer limit of their range decreases, but that in some cases this relationship is absent. This combination also appears to accord closely with Christaller's assumptions about the distribution of population.

Some characteristics of the K3 system of central places

When fully developed the L-system of central places is characterised by a specific ratio of the number of places in successive orders. The ratio of L : P : G : B : K : A : M-places is $1 : 2 : 6 : 18 : 54 : 162 : 486$. This ratio is constant throughout the system and is equally applicable to G- or A-systems, viz., $1 : 2 : 6 : 18$ and $1 : 2$, respectively. More

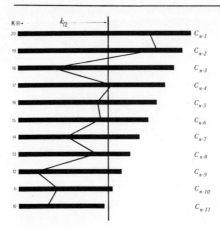

Fig. 3.19   Relationship between threshold as a random proportion of the outer limit of the range of a commodity C_α. The amount of excess profits, indicated by the distance between the irregular and leftward trending line and the real limit of the range (vertical line) varies for successively lower order commodities (from Beavon, op. cit., 15, 1975).

generally, the ratio of $1:2:6:18:54$, etc., is applicable to the ratio of the highest order place to next higher order places to next higher, etc. This is readily verified by examining Fig. 3.10. There is only one G-place. At the boundary of the G-region there are six B-places, but only one-third of each B-place falls within the G-system giving a total of two G-places. There are six K-places. There are twelve A-places wholly within the boundaries of the G-region and a further twelve that lie athwart the boundary, yielding only a half of each of them to the G-system shown; hence a total of eighteen A-places. Similarly, there are fifty-four M-places.

Vertical and horizontal order

Within the K3 central place system there is both a *vertical* and *horizontal* regularity. In the latter case the regularity manifests itself in terms of both the distance between, and relative locations of, places of different orders in any direction. This should already be clear from the data shown in Tables 3.1 and 3.2. The vertical order refers to the internal composition and characteristic role of each central place. From the discussion already presented, it is clear that a place of any order offers all the commodities offered by a place of immediate lower order plus a set of commodities that distinguishes it from the lower order place. A popular interpretation, manifest by those that support the assumption that the extent of the threshold is a constant proportion of the outer limit of the range of a commodity, is that the highest order commodity offered by a place is necessarily that commodity which has the outer limit of its range equal to the range of the region of that place. In considering the range of a region it should be clear from the explanation offered that this is not the case. The reason is that Christaller's central place system was based on the outer limit of the range of a commodity and not on the inner limit (a fact indicated correctly in two of the general texts now available, viz., Murphy, 1966, pp. 74–5, and Carter, 1972, pp. 72–4). The outer limit of the range of a commodity can obviously be greater than the range of the region of the place from which the commodity is offered (cf., Fig. 3.16). However, provided the threshold area necessary to support the commodity is less than the area of the region, as demarcated by the range of the region, the commodity can be offered and earn at least normal profits.

Relationship to the theory of tertiary activity

The similarity between what has been deduced from Christaller's model, based on the assumption that threshold requirements are proportional to the outer limit of the range of a commodity, and the later extension of central place theory to the theory of tertiary activity, should now be apparent. Consider Table 3.3 As already shown, the threshold requirements for various commodities are likely to be met from small threshold areas. As such, the excess profit situation for all C_n commodities will occur without necessarily assuming that the extent of the threshold is a constant proportion of the outer limit of the range of a commodity. Furthermore it

Table 3.3   The supply of commodities C_n to C_1 by seven orders of central place (from Beavon, op. cit., 15, 1975).

Type of central place						
L (7)	P (6)	G (5)	B (4)	K (3)	A (2)	M (1)
n†‡§						
$n-1$	$n-1$§					
$n-2$	$n-2$					
...	...					
...	...					
$n-i$†	$n-i$‡					
$n-(i+1)$	$n-(i+1)$	$n-(i+1)$§				
...	...	...				
...	...	...				
$n-j$†	$n-j$	$n-j$‡				
$n-(j+1)$	$n-(j+1)$	$n-(j+1)$	$n-(j+1)$§			
...	...	...	...			
...	...	...	...			
$n-k$†	$n-k$	$n-k$	$n-k$‡			
$n-(k+1)$	$n-(k+1)$	$n-(k+1)$	$n-(k+1)$	$n-(k+1)$§		
...	...	...	...	...		
...	...	...	...	...		
$n-l$†	$n-l$	$n-l$	$n-l$	$n-l$‡		
$n-(l+1)$	$n-(l+1)$	$n-(l+1)$	$n-(l+1)$	$n-(l+1)$	$n-(l+1)$§	
...	...	...	...	...	...	
...	...	...	...	...	...	
$n-m$†	$n-m$	$n-m$	$n-m$	$n-m$	$n-m$	$n-m$‡
$n-(m+1)$	$n-(m+1)$	$n-(m+1)$	$n-(m+1)$	$n-(m+1)$	$n-(m+1)$	$n-(m+1)$§
...	...	...	...	...	...	...
...	...	...	...	...	...	$n-(m+x)$‡
...	...	...	...	...	...	...
1	1	1	1	1	1	1

† Represents that commodity that can just be offered to all parts of the region from existing centres. Corresponds to the *marginal hierarchical good* of the theory of tertiary activity.
‡ Represents the commodity that determines the *range of the region* of the particular central place.
§ Represents the highest order commodity offered from a particular central place. The order of the commodity is proportional to its outer limit range.

should be noted that the commodities of an order higher than that corresponding to the *marginal hierarchical commodity* (*good*) are offered from each order of central place. This is directly attributable to the fact that Christaller does not develop his system on the basis of thresholds. Consequently the *range of region* of any central place does not specify the maximum threshold population for all commodities offered from it.

It has been shown how the system of central places has emerged as a result of the work of Christaller based on the expressed ideas and work of previous researchers. More specifically it has been shown how the system of central places, developed according to the marketing principle, can be deduced in a general way without recourse to the specific distance values employed in the original work. In re-examining this aspect of Christaller's work, it has become clear that a discrepancy exists between what he actually stated and what is commonly believed by others to have been stated. The most important finding is that Christaller does not, and need not, assume an isotropic plane for the development of his central place systems. It is sufficient to assume a homogeneous transportation surface with a regular but not necessarily even distribution of population, concentrated in and about the urban places and dispersed more thinly through the countryside. As a result, Christaller is able to assume small threshold *areas*. The emergence of the hierarchical scale of central places on the basis of the outer limit of the range of a commodity is dependent on the servicing requirement of the model, viz., all areas should be supplied with all commodities offered by the highest order central place but all commodities have a finite range beyond which they cannot be distributed. Thus the locations of central places *emerge* and are *not assumed* in the first instance: this is in contradistinction to the work of Lösch to be discussed in the second part of this book. The economic domain of the conventional cost and revenue curves emerges as a ring between the inner and outer limits of the range of a commodity and represents the spatial projection of net profits for that commodity. Thus, excess profits are available within the system and the *amount* of such profits depends on the varying assumptions that can be made about the relationship between threshold area, population distribution, and the outer limit of the range of a commodity. However, it has been shown that the popularly held assumption that the extent of the threshold bears a constant proportional relationship to the outer limit of the range of a commodity is in conflict with Christaller's assumed regular but uneven distribution of population. The similarity between the Christaller system of central places and that of the theory of tertiary activity has been briefly demonstrated. Thus armed with hindsight it should be clear that the latter system cannot be seen to represent anything greatly different from that contained in the original work of Christaller.

Thus, implicit in the central place system of Christaller is the capacity for businesses to earn both excess and normal profits. By developing the system in the manner described in this chapter, but *within* a metropolitan region, the composition of the stepped hierarchy of Christaller can readily be interpreted on the *intra*-urban level. Therefore, although the reasoning on which the theory of tertiary activity is based appears to have certain shortcomings, it has now been shown that the same effective intra-urban hierarchy can be deduced from the original work of Christaller. Thus on theoretical grounds, and in terms of the structural component, there appears no reason for not accepting a central place theory that postulates a stepped hierarchy of shopping centres.

Allied to both the theory of tertiary activity and the original central place theory, but not yet discussed in detail, are certain techniques for recognising hierarchies in practice. The nature of the techniques adopted and the role they have played in the classificatory process now deserves consideration.

Notes

1. The idea that an urban place is a *central place*, a focus for a variety of different human activities serving the surrounding countryside, was introduced to English-language geographical literature in 1931 by Jefferson (1931, p. 453). It is believed that this was the first use of the term *central place* (Dickinson, 1964, p. 49), and as such pre-dates by two years the use of the term by Christaller himself. Nevertheless, it is the work of Christaller from which central place theory stems and with which the term *central place* is most readily associated.

2. Of the English-language geographers, James A. Barnes was possibly the first to become familiar with the work of Christaller, although that honour is normally accorded to Ullman (1941). A paper by Barnes and Robinson (1940) indicates that they were at least aware of Christaller's work although they make no specific reference to him. Both Wehrwein (1942) and Trewartha (1943), when making use of a diagram showing aspects of Christaller's central place system, give acknowledgement to J. A. Barnes but without reference details.

3. The term *central place*, as adopted by Christaller in 1933, is derived not from Jefferson's (1931) work but from the earlier statement in German that the prime function of a *town* is to be the 'centre of its rural surroundings and mediator of local commerce with the outside world' (Gradmann, 1916, p. 427).

4. In the translated version the terms *goods* and *functions* appear. For clarity these are replaced here with the terms *commodities* and *activities* or *businesses* respectively.

5. Attention has been drawn by Muller and Diaz (1973) to a similar misrepresentation of the work of Von Thünen in publications by Horvath (1969), Yeates and Garner (1971), Webber (1972), and Angel and Hyman (1972). Whereas Von Thünen makes use of a uniform transportation surface, this has been misinterpreted as an isotropic surface. It is only the latter surface that possesses the *additional* attribute of an even distribution of population (Hägerstrand, 1965).

6. Saey (1973, p. 184) has also drawn attention to this misinterpretation.

7. The highest and second highest order places, L- and P-places respectively, were introduced only at a later stage. The prefix letters stand for the terms associated with typical places in the observed hierarchy in southern Germany, viz.: G *Gaustadt* (small state capital); B *Bezirksstadt* (district city); K *Kreisstadt* (county seat); A *Amtsort* (township centre); M *Marktort* (market hamlet) (Ullman, 1941).

8. The statement 'at least three *other* central places' (author's italics) (Christaller, 1966, p. 61) is only correct if it is assumed that having established the first central place (B′) it is desired to supply the unsupplied ring. Certainly as shown in Fig. 3.8 the whole area supplied by B′ can be supplied by B_1, B_2, and B_3 without B′ being necessary. The implication contained in the original work must be that once a central place is established (on the theoretical plane) it remains fixed and operative at that location.

9. If population is evenly distributed *and if* the *inner limit* of the range of the commodities is greater than $k\sqrt{3}$ the circles describing such ranges about K-places will overlap and effectively exclude their supply. However, as the distribution of population is probably such that there is an agglomeration in the towns (Christaller, 1966, pp. 60, 66, 67), the *threshold area*, defined by the inner limit of the range, will probably have a smaller radius.

10. If the argument set out in the preceding pages commenced with a P′-place instead of a B′-place, the five successively lower order places and the higher order L-place could be derived in the same manner. For purely comparative purposes the general procedure set out above has commenced at the level of the B′-place. The prefix letters P and L stand for *Provinzhauptstadt* and *Landeshauptstadt* respectively.

11. It has been suggested (Ullman, 1941) that the distance of 4 km i.e., the range of region for M-places, was chosen by Christaller because 4—5 km, approximately the distance that can be walked in an hour, appears to be a normal service area limit for the smallest centre, given the particular technology of the time in Germany.

12. Christaller first employed the idea of a socio-political principle that he termed a separation principle. The term administrative principle also used by Christaller is now the best-known term for the K7 system of central places (cf., Christaller, 1966, p. 77).

13. This corresponds with the case of commodities Number 21 and 20, with outer limits of the range equal to 21 and 20 km respectively (Christaller, 1966, pp. 61–2).

14. This corresponds with commodity Number 12 with an outer limit of the range of 12 km (Christaller, 1966, p. 62).

15. The outer limit of the range of commodity C_{n-10} and lower order commodities offered from K- and B-places are less than the real limit between the two places.

16. As the present discussion is only concerned with the implied relationship between a K- and B-place it is inappropriate to consider commodities of lower order than C_{n-9}. Commodity C_{n-10} is the highest order commodity offered from the next higher order place, an A-place (Fig. 3.16c, b). As such, commodity C_{n-10} must be viewed in the same way as commodity C_n in Fig. 3.16a. By substituting K for B, A for K, and M for A in Fig. 3.16, the diagram can be used to study the relationships, now under discussion, for lower levels of the system of central places.

17. The figure of 52.5 per cent is only applicable if the decrease in the outer limit of the range of a commodity is in accordance with the assumption expressed in equation 3.9. In the general case the percentage can be calculated from $R'_j/k - d_j$ where R'_j is the real range of the jth order central place, k is the distance between the j and $(j-1)$th order central place, and d_j is the difference between the outer limits of the range of the highest order commodity offered by the $(j-1)$th order central place and the next highest order commodity.

Chapter 4

The classification of urban hierarchies

Three broad approaches to the classification of central places are recognised: a two-parameter approach based on the number of businesses of a central place and the population they serve; multivariate statistical procedures of which the factor analytic approach has been the most common; and an approach based on indices of centrality.

Traditional approaches

The two-parameter approach

The identification of groups of central places, using bi-variate data and the Clark and Evans (1954) definition of a group is an often-used procedure in identifying inter- and intra-urban hierarchical groups (e.g., Berry and Garrison, 1958a; King, 1962; Johnston, 1966; Berry, 1967; R. J. Davies, 1967). The major shortcoming of this procedure lies in the imprecise nature of the Clark and Evans definition[1] and the resultant inconsistency of its application. The definition is based on the concept that every member of a group should be closer to some other member of the group than to some other point. It is not clear whether individuals have used it to distinguish between either horizontal, vertical or diagonal distances on scattergrams or whether they have used the more abstract informational distance between places in the distribution (Hall, 1969a). Consequently it has been concluded that the recognition of finite groups of places by this approach is doubtful (King, 1962, p. 148). In addition the second parameter, i.e., population served by a central place, is difficult to measure with the accuracy that the approach implies.

Certainly within urban areas the measurement of the population served by a central place, i.e., a shopping centre, is synonymous with the determination of a trade area. Various shopping models of the gravity type have been developed to approximate the population that would be drawn to a shopping centre under various assumptions of the attractive power of the shopping centre. Even the most sophisticated models are only able to approximate the trade population of a shopping centre. This is clearly indicative of the caution that needs to be exercised if a single population figure is used as a parameter of a particular shopping centre, in a set of shopping centres, to be classified as part of a hierarchy using a scattergram. The difficulty of measuring intra-urban trade areas is probably the reason why even the theory of tertiary activity was initially tested on empirical data relating to sets of small to moderate sized towns in rural regions. The analogy that towns in a region are comparable to shopping centres in a metropolitan region has obviously

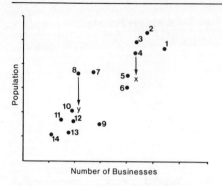

Fig. 4.1   A hypothetical set of places arranged on a scattergram in terms of their population and number of businesses.

been made. So too has the additional assumption been made that the population of a district about a rural service centre is the population served by that service centre.

The possible effect of inaccurate population figures coupled with a particular interpretation of the Clark and Evans definition of a group can be illustrated graphically. Consider the hypothetical set of fourteen central places arranged on a scattergram (Fig. 4.1). On the assumption that the 'distance' referred to by Clark and Evans is measurable in any direction, it is possible to make out a case for three groups of central places viz.:

Group A containing places 1 to 4,
Group B containing places 5 to 8, and
Group C containing places 9 to 14.

Suppose that the population parameters of places 4 and 8 had been incorrectly measured and the revised measurements place them at points X and Y respectively (Fig. 4.1). The case could now be argued for three groups composed as follows:

Group A containing places 1 to 3,
Group B containing places 4 to 7, and
Group C containing places 8 to 14.

Apart from the fact that interpretation is subjective, the scattergrams to which this form of cluster recognition has been applied must have given the individual researchers considerable problems. Consider the two examples shown in Figs 4.2 and 4.3. Only by the most precise measurement could R. J. Davies (1967) have made the divisions between the orders 5 through to 7 for the South African towns in his data set (Fig. 4.2). Indeed R. J. Davies (1967, p. 13) states that it may be argued that the distribution is more accurately a continuum. Furthermore, he states that strict application of the Clark and Evans definition will identify distinct sub-groups within the eight groups recognised. In a similar example (Fig. 4.3) Barnum (1966) identifies a five-level hierarchy in Southern Germany. He too makes a state-ment (Barnum, 1966, p. 42) that the scattergram indicates an overall continuum. Nevertheless, using a similar approach to that employed by other adherents of the two-parameter approach, five levels of a hierarchy are recognised.

The application of the two-parameter approach and the use of a scattergram has, however, revealed more distinct and relatively less controversial groupings. For

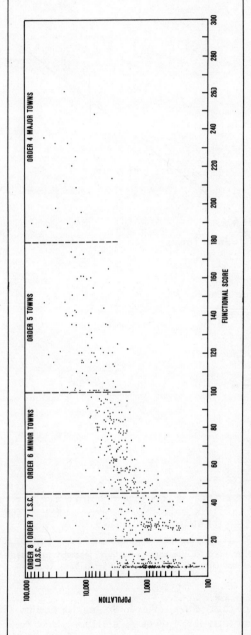

Fig. 4.2   The scattergram used in establishing the South African urban hierarchy (after R. J. Davies, *S. Afr. Geog. J.*, 49, 1967).

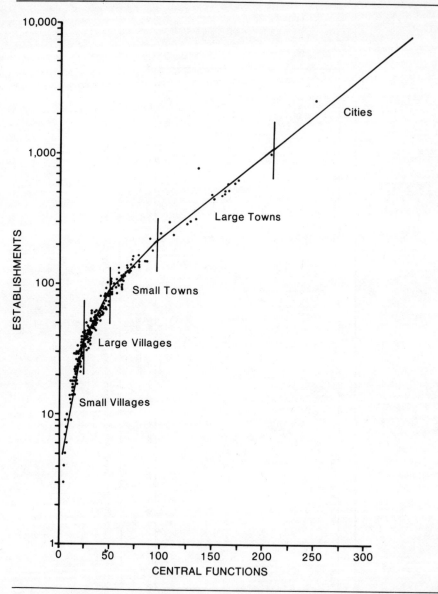

Fig. 4.3 The scattergram used to illustrate the urban hierarchy in Baden–Württemberg (after Barnum, *Market Centres and Hinterlands in Baden–Württemberg*, 1966).

example, the study of thirty-three towns in Snohomish County (cf., Fig. 2.1), and King's (1962) study of forty-three towns in Canterbury, New Zealand (Fig. 4.4).

Given the relationship between population served and number of businesses as postulated in equation 2.1, viz.,

$$P = A(B^N)$$

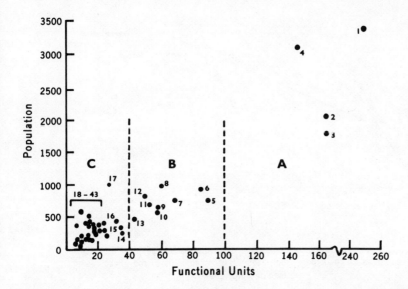

Fig. 4.4 The scattergram used to illustrate the relative relationships of small towns in Canterbury, New Zealand. The numbers assist in making a comparison with the dendrogram of Fig. 4.10 (after King, *Proc. Third N.Z. Geog. Conf.*, 1962).

it follows that for ease of graphical representation the logarithm of the population of central places is plotted against the number of businesses. Hierarchical groups of central places have also been recognised by the fitting of a series of regression equations to such bivariate distributions through the largely subjective selection of breaks in the slope of the overall distribution. Examples include a study of central places in Tasmania (Scott, 1964), a study in Baden–Württenberg (Barnum, 1966) and a study of Chicago (Garner, 1966) (Figs 4.5, 4.3 and 4.6 respectively). This particular approach has been severely criticised by Johnston (1964) who argues that the use of a semilogarithmic graph transforms a non-linear relationship on an arithmetic graph into a linear relationship. To fit linear regression lines to a number of apparent breaks in the slope of the transformed scatter can affect the interpretation of the data. At the time that this criticism was voiced, however, the existence of a hierarchy was not questioned, the technique of recognising it was.

Yet a third variation of the two-parameter approach to classification has been based on the use of oblique axes and standard scores (based on Rao, 1948). Both King (1962) and Johnston (1966) have used this variation (Figs 4.7, 4.8) but are agreed that the recognition of groups is subjective. Indeed the recognition of eight hierarchical orders in the intra-metropolitan system of Melbourne (Fig. 4.8) clearly indicates that the boundary lines could have been determined after only the most precise measurements in the application of the Clark and Evans definition of a group. The existence of a continuum of points representing shopping centres in Melbourne is most striking.

The studies reported in the above section represent examples of the application of the two-parameter approach to the classification of urban hierarchies. An interesting feature that has emerged in the discussion so far should again be noted.

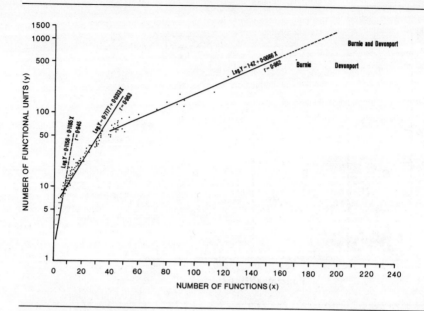

Fig. 4.5 The semi-logarithmic scattergram and associated regression lines used in establishing the hierarchy of central places in Tasmania (after Scott, *Austr. Geog., 9, 1964*).

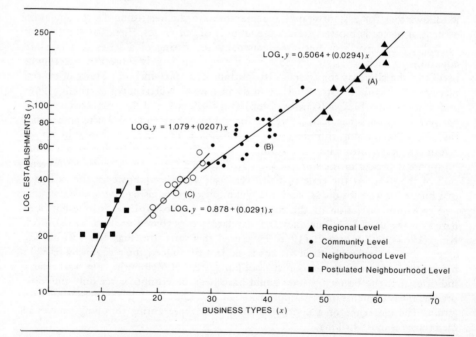

Fig. 4.6 The semi-logarithmic scattergram and associated regression lines used in the study of the intra-urban hierarchy of Chicago (after Garner, *The Internal Structure of Retail Nucleations, 1966*).

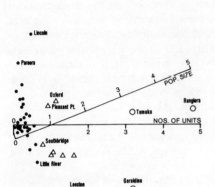

Fig. 4.7   The scattergram of New Zealand towns arranged relative to a set of rotated axes. The angle θ between the axes is given by the relationship $cos\ \theta = r_{xy}$. On the Y-axis (population size) one unit represents 731 persons, on the X-axis one unit represents fifty-three businesses (after King, *Proc. Third N.Z. Geog. Conf.*, 1962).

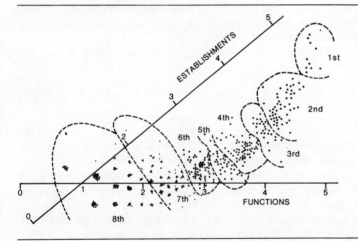

Fig. 4.8   The scattergram of 718 shopping centres in Melbourne arranged relative to rotated axes. Smaller dots have been used in the seventh and eighth order zones for cartographic convenience only (after Johnston, *Austr. Geog. Stud.*, 4, 1966).

Whereas in almost all cases cited in this chapter a continuum appeared and was recognised as such, hierarchical breaks were nevertheless sought and established! The significance of this is discussed at the end of this chapter.

Multivariate statistical techniques

In an attempt to develop an alternative classificatory procedure the relevance of accurate population data as a *sine qua non* has also been questioned by Abiodun (1967). In advocating a multivariate approach Abiodun has opted for the use of factor analytic procedures for establishing hierarchical groups in central place systems (as had Berry and Barnum, 1962; Berry *et al.*, 1962). However, the work of Abiodun based on a Nigerian example has been questioned, on the grounds that it was a stated intention of the study to produce a hierarchy of places for the area studied. More generally the appropriateness of the complex analytical procedure has been questioned given the relative crudity and variability of the input data (Carter, 1972, p. 97). In the Nigerian study it is made clear that data on retail establishments was not readily available for all business types. Hence only 'representative' data was employed (Abiodun, 1967, p. 351). It has been pointed out (Carter, 1972, p. 97) that as a result the data in the Nigerian study is not only preselected but the grounds of preselection are subjective and unknown. Furthermore Carter (1972) takes the Nigerian study to task for using a technique with the intention of affecting the ease with which the groups in the hierarchy could be recognised.

As a result of the awareness of this type of criticism the use of centrality indices have been favoured by some.

Centrality indices

Several centrality indices have been developed and used since 1965 (W. K. Davies, 1965, 1967, 1968; R. J. Davies, 1967; McEvoy, 1968; Dutt, 1969; Marshall, 1969; Lewis, 1970; Rowley, 1970; Preston, 1971). Of those referenced here that of Wayne Davies appears to have attracted the most use.

Davies' measure of centrality is a modification of the industrial location coefficient and may be defined as

$$C_t = \frac{100}{T} \tag{4.1}$$

where C_t is the centrality value for any particular type of commodity t, and T is the total number of business establishments for commodity t. In applying the location coefficient it is first necessary to calculate the particular C_t values for each commodity t and then to multiply the number of establishments observed in the place under study by the appropriate C_t value. This yields the amount of centrality conferred on each place by each business type. Summation of the individual centrality indices in turn yields an overall index of centrality for each place studied. It is this final figure that is termed the *functional index* by Davies.

Although the functional index is a relatively unsophisticated index in its raw form, it can be modified to take into account the variation in the size of a particular business establishment of type t. This has been done by the relatively simple expedient of introducing a weighting for the number of persons employed or floor space occupied (Davies, W. K., 1965, p. 224). The main disadvantage of both the modified and simple functional indices is that a closed system of central places is presupposed (Carter, 1972, p. 98). Other centrality indices vary in their complexity and make varying demand for data that is not universally available and readily collected. Two examples can be considered.

The first is the hierarchic index developed in a case study of Calcutta (Dutt, 1969). The measure termed the *composite hierarchic level* or *CHL* is defined as:

$$CHL = \frac{1,000(X_i)}{A} + \frac{1,000(Y_i)}{B} \tag{4.2}$$

where A is the sum of customers using a market (i.e., the population served), B is the sum of the market areas from which consumers are attracted (i.e., the trade area), X_i is the number of customers shopping in a market place i, and Y_i is the catchment area of market place i. Clearly the data required presupposes a sophisticated data retrieval system. In passing, the thought must arise whether such an index could be successfully employed in a developed country let alone in a developing country.

In attempting to measure centrality Christaller developed his own centrality index. It is based on the assumption that the hierarchical status of a town can be inferred from its sphere of influence. The measure Christaller adopted was designed to show just this and incorporated the use of telephones. It is essential to remember that at the time the index was developed the telephone was not the ubiquitous instrument that it has now become. The measure of centrality Z_z (Christaller, 1966, pp. 143–50) is given below:

$$Z_z = T_z - E_z \frac{T_g}{E_g} \tag{4.3}$$

where T_z is the number of telephones in the central place, E_z the population of the central place, T_g the number of telephones in the region (e.g., a B-region) and E_g the population of the region. The measure Z_z gives the relative concentration of telephones in the central place compared to the region served. Obviously the use of the telephone as an appropriate indicator of centrality is today no longer quite as valid. In an attempt to operationalise Christaller's concept of centrality Preston (1971) has proposed the following index of centrality C:

$$C = R + S - \alpha MF \tag{4.4}$$

where R is the total sales made in retail establishments, S is the total sales in service establishments, α is the average percentage of median family income spent on retail items and selected [*sic*] services by family units in a central place, M is the median family income for a central place and F is the total number of families in a central place. The data requirements for the Preston centrality index are also stringent and must preclude the widespread use of the index notwithstanding its conceptual appeal.

Whereas the calculation of the centrality indices in general requires only minor manipulation of the required data, the identification of groups of central places remains subjective and unresolved. The problem of recognising breaks in the ranked index values requires a technique not only for recognising the break but for assessing whether such a break is of sufficient magnitude to constitute a break between groups of ranked central places.

The reader will have noticed that certain conflicts have once again become apparent. On the one hand there is a desire to make grouping procedures in central place studies relatively simple and objective. On the other hand there appears to be a desire to definitely identify a hierarchy. The latter desire appears to be in conflict with the first, but only if it is recognised that hierarchies of the type identified by both central place theory and the theory of tertiary activity may not exist. This latter viewpoint appears in turn to conflict with central place theory as till recently enunciated. Marshall (1969) for example makes use of the functional index and in so doing attempts to clarify the definition of a group. This is done in such a way as to make allowance for central places that do not fit into *perfectly hierarchical systems* (Marshall, 1969, pp. 92–3) to be regarded as *essentially* hierarchical. Furthermore, a set of such places can be classified as part of an *imperfect hierarchical system* 'if it can be made to satisfy [criteria] by arbitrary adjustment of the centrality values' (Marshall, 1969, p. 93).

In view of the over-interpretation that can become possible when a fixed definition of a group is too assiduously applied a more cautious procedure is indicated. It would be preferable in interpreting the results of grouping procedures to adopt an approach in which the grouping or absence thereof is established on the basis of logical argument. This would appear to be acceptable in view of the opinion that classification is a subjective process although the actual methodology may be based on objective numerical procedures (Lambert and Dale, 1964, p. 62; Johnston, 1968a, p. 588). Even the use of statistical significance for recognising the best number of groups has been queried (Labovitz, 1968; Johnston, 1970).

The multivariate approach reassessed

The attractive feature of the multivariate approach is that grouping can be based on raw data matrices representing the composition and number of businesses present in a set of central places. However, fundamental to the whole grouping procedure is the measure of similarity that is employed. Factor analytical procedures involve the use of product–moment correlation coefficients based on normal or normalised data. As much of the data that is used in classificatory stages of central place analysis is either skew or difficult to normalise, it has been suggested that there is a need to develop more generalised multidimensional measures of similarity as a preliminary to grouping procedures (Spence and Taylor, 1970). In heeding the suggestion by Spence and Taylor the field of numerical taxonomy has proved both fertile and stimulating. It is however necessary to proceed with caution.

An alternative measure of similarity

A geotaxonomic approach to the classification of central places has been adopted by Beavon and Hall (1972). The approach is based on the maxim that a satisfactory measure of similarity must ensure that every item contributes to the homogeneity or similarity index in such a way that there will be no undue weighting within the data matrix comprising items (e.g., shopping centres, administrative regions) and properties (e.g., types of shop, employment categories). Secondly, each property should contribute independently to the measure of similarity, to ensure that groups are maximally homogeneous for the greatest number of properties. Two measures that meet these requirements are the relative heterogeneity (H_q) and the frequency modulated relative homogeneity (H'_{qm}) functions (Hall, 1967, 1969a, b; Beavon and Hall, 1972).

The detailed derivation of the functions and the description of the associated space-conserving calculated average member clustering algorithm have been presented elsewhere (Beavon and Hall, 1972; Brundrit, 1972; Beavon, 1974c). For the purposes of discussion here it is sufficient to present the equations that describe the two functions and their relationship to each other. Reference can be made to the general form of the data matrix shown as Table 4.1.

Table 4.1 General form of the data matrix. If used for grouping shopping centres different types of businesses appear as properties 1, 2, ..., p, and shopping centres are represented as items 1,..., i, j, ... n. For dichotomous data only zeros and ones denoting absence and presence, will be entered. Alternatively, the observed number of businesses per business type per shopping centre can be entered at the appropriate position in the matrix.

Property	Item				
	1	...	$i, ... j,$	...	n
1	a_{11}	...	$a_{i1} ... a_{j1}$	...	a_{n1}
2	a_{12}	...	$a_{i2} ... a_{j2}$	...	a_{n2}
.					
.					
.					
q	a_{1q}	...	$a_{iq} ... a_{jq}$	...	a_{nq}
.					
.					
p	a_{1p}	...	$a_{ip} ... a_{jp}$	...	a_{np}

Relative heterogeneity

The relative heterogeneity H_q of i samples averaged over p properties is

$$H_q = \frac{1}{p} \sum_{j=1}^{p} \frac{\sigma_{jn}}{\sigma_{jnb}} \tag{4.5}$$

where σ_{jn} is the standard deviation of the values for a particular property across a set of items and σ_{jnb} is the same for the standard group with maximum heterogeneity.

Whereas the procedure outlined above is suitable for dichotomous data, geographers deal most frequently with ratio data. In such circumstances the H_q function reduces to a simple modulus when the relative heterogeneity for a pair of items x and y is calculated. For a property j that has been scaled to unity[2] the function is:

$$H_q = \frac{1}{p} \sum_{j=1}^{p} |a_{jx} - a_{jy}| \tag{4.6}$$

where a_{jx} and a_{jy} represent the scaled values of the original data for x and y as scored on property j. The H_q function resembles the *Mean Character Difference* of Cain and Harrison (1958) derived on different grounds. The form of H_q given in equation 4.6 is particularly useful in computing a similarity matrix of all possible pairs of items. It is preferable to the taxonomic distance measure d where larger differences between property values for any pair of items tend to be overemphasised in the process of being squared before addition (Hall, 1969b; Beavon and Hall, 1972). This is shown for some data sets in Table 4.2. It will be noticed that the differences between results obtained by H_q and d are not exceptionally

Table 4.2 A comparison of results for the relative heterogeneity function H_q and the taxonomic distance measure d using hypothetical data (reprinted from 'A Geotaxonomic Approach to Classification in Urban and Regional Studies,' by K. S. O. Beavon and A. V. Hall, *Geographical Analysis*, Vol. 4, No. 4 (October 1972), 407−15. Copyright © 1972 by the Ohio State University Press).

Property row j	Scaled data (a) for two items, x and y		$H_q = \dfrac{1}{p} \sum\limits_{j=1}^{p} \|a_{jx} - a_{jy}\|$	$d = \left[\dfrac{1}{p} \sum\limits_{j=1}^{p} (a_{jx} - a_{jy})^2 \right]^{\frac{1}{2}}$
1	0.1	1.0	½(0.9 + 0.1)	[½(0.81 + 0.01)]$^{\frac{1}{2}}$
2	0.1	0.2	= 0.50	= 0.64
1	0.1	0.5	½(0.4 + 0.1)	[½(0.16 + 0.01)]$^{\frac{1}{2}}$
2	0.1	0.2	= 0.25	= 0.29
1	0.1	0.3	½(0.2 + 0.1)	[½(0.04 + 0.01)]$^{\frac{1}{2}}$
2	0.1	0.2	= 0.15	= 0.16
1	0.1	0.2	½(0.1 + 0.1)	[½(0.01 + 0.01)]$^{\frac{1}{2}}$
2	0.1	0.2	= 0.10	= 0.10
1	0.1	1.0	½(0.9 + 0.1 + 0.1)	[½(0.81 + 0.01 + 0.01)]$^{\frac{1}{2}}$
2	0.1	0.2	= 0.37	= 0.53
3	0.1	0.2		

large. However, although its semi-geometric derivation may be attractive, the taxonomic distance function has distortions that make it undesirable, a view also put forward by Colless (1967). Relative homogeneity H'_q is given by

$$H'_q = 1 - H_q \tag{4.7}$$

Frequency modulated relative homogeneity

In order to emphasise similarity among the property rows that have higher scores the frequency modulated relative homogeneity function H'_{qm} is best used. For a set of k items and $j = 1 \ldots p$ properties H'_{qm} is given by

$$H'_{qm} = \sum_{j=1}^{p} \left[\left(\sum_{t=1}^{k} a_{jt} \right) \left(\sum_{j=1}^{p} \sum_{t=1}^{k} a_{jt} \right)^{-1} \right] \left[1 - \frac{\sigma_{jk}}{\sigma_{jkb}} \right] \tag{4.8}$$

H'_{qm} can be rewritten for ease of computing[3] a similarity matrix for all possible pairs of items. Thus for a set of t to k items and $j = 1 \ldots p$ properties, H'_{qm} is given by

$$H'_{qm} = \sum_{j=1}^{p} \left[\frac{a_{jt} + a_{jk}}{\sum\limits_{j=1}^{p} (a_{jt} + a_{jk})} \right] \left[1 - |a'_{jt} - a'_{jk}| \right] \tag{4.9}$$

where a_{jt} and a_{jk} are the scores of property j for items t and k respectively. The primed variables (a') indicate scaled property data. The first expression in square brackets serves to give the frequency modulating factor. The homogeneity is found by the second expression in square brackets where the absolute difference between

Table 4.3 Hypothetical scaled data for two items *t* and *k* with six properties (reprinted from 'A Geotaxonomic Approach to Classification in Urban and Regional Studies,' by K. S. O. Beavon and A. V. Hall, *Geographical Analysis*, Vol. 4, No. 4 (October 1972), 407–15. Copyright © 1972 by the Ohio State University Press).

Property row	Scaled data for two items		Modulating factor, M	Homogeneity value, H'	MH'
	t	*k*			
1	0.0	0.0	0.0/5.8 = 0	1.0	0.00
2	1.0	1.0	2.0/5.8 = 0.35	1.0	0.35
3	0.1	0.1	0.2/5.8 = 0.04	1.0	0.04
4	0.6	0.4	1.0/5.8 = 0.17	0.8	0.14
5	0.0	1.0	1.0/5.8 = 0.17	0.0	0.00
6	0.8	0.8	1.6/5.8 = 0.28	1.0	0.28
				$\Sigma MH' = H'_{qm} =$	0.81

the scaled values for a given property is subtracted from unity. The calculation of H'_{qm} for a set of items *t* and *k* is shown in Table 4.3.

Determining intra-urban hierarchies

The H'_{qm} measure can be used to recognise the internal structural relationships of a set of central places. As such it can indicate the existence of either a continuum or a hierarchy. To illustrate the use of the technique a hypothetical example of a hierarchy will first be examined. The classification procedure and its results can then be compared with a more traditional method for the same example.

Classifying shopping centres

Consider the following example. Suppose data relating to a number of different types of shops were collected in four shopping centres, A, B, C, D, which are known to serve exactly 400, 450, 1,200 and 1,000 people respectively (Table 4.4). When this data is plotted on a scatter diagram (Fig. 4.9a) the points A and B are shown to be very close to each other. Normally they would be interpreted as being members of a single group in the hierarchy and C and D could be regarded as representative of two other levels. However, suppose that examination of the

Table 4.4 Hypothetical population totals and occurrence of business types in four intra-metropolitan shopping centres (after Beavon, *S. Afr. Geog. J.*, **52**, 1970b).

Business types	Centres			
	A	B	C	D
Clothing shops	1	1	5	4
Butcher shops	1	1	2	2
Food shops	3	3	4	3
Pharmacies	1	1	2	1
Cafés	1	1	1	1
Total number of shops	7	7	14	11
Population served	400	450	1,200	1,000

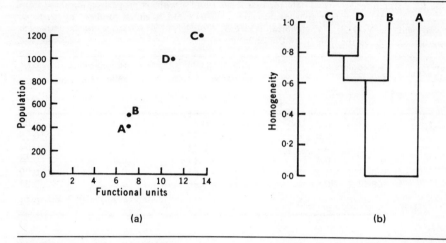

(a)   (b)

Fig. 4.9   (a) Relationships between four hypothetical centres on the basis of total number of businesses and population served by each. (b) Association between the same centres when qualitative differences are included and grouping is based on homogeneity values (from Beavon, op. cit., 52, 1970b).

on-ground situation reveals that for each of the business types, listed above and found in centres B, C, and D, the shops are modern, clean and in a good state of repair. In the case of centre A the shops are all in a poor state of repair and are functionally impaired by dated shopfittings. Intuitively it can be accepted that such a centre must be regarded as of a different type to that of centre B, although they have the identical number of shops in each of the business types present.

If a distinction is made between centres that are functionally and/or physically desirable (I) and those that are functionally and physically blighted (II) (following Berry, 1963, p. 195), then Table 4.4 can be rearranged to give the data matrix shown in Table 4.5. This rearrangement does not affect the total number of businesses per centre nor the population they serve. However, when used as the input in the frequency modulated relative homogeneity function the classification is very

Table 4.5   Hypothetical occurrence of two grades of business types in the four intra-metropolitan shopping centres (after Beavon, op. cit., 52, 1970b).

Business types	Grade	Centres			
		A	B	C	D
Clothing shops	I	0	1	5	4
Clothing shops	II	1	0	0	0
Butcher shops	I	0	1	2	2
Butcher shops	II	1	0	0	0
Food shops	I	0	3	4	3
Food shops	II	3	0	0	0
Pharmacies	I	0	1	2	1
Pharmacies	II	1	0	0	0
Cafés	I	0	1	1	1
Cafés	II	1	0	0	0

different from that derived from the scatter diagram. The linkages and the homogeneity levels at which such linkages take place are:

C links to D at a homogeneity level of 0.798,
B links to CD group at a homogeneity level of 0.613, and
A links to the CDB group at a homogeneity level of zero.

The association between A, B, C and D is shown in Fig. 4.9b. Interpretation of the dendrogram shows that centres C and D are very similar, that centre B is much closer in composition to the average of group C and D than it is to centre A. Centre A, that is totally different from centre B, is shown by the homogeneity value of zero to also be totally different from the group CDB.

The use of the homogeneity function provides the basis of like-grouping of central places. The number of groups decreases from the n individual centres (or n groups) at a homogeneity level of 1.0 to a single group at a level somewhere between 0 and 1.0. Consequently at any specified homogeneity level it is possible to compare an individual member of one group with an individual member of another group.

It is important to note that the dendrogram merely shows the resemblance between individual centres and groups of centres but does not in itself indicate the rank of a group. Notwithstanding, those centres with a greater number of businesses and greater variety of business types will tend to be the higher order centres and will be more heterogeneous than smaller centres. As such the link levels of higher order centres will tend to be at lower levels of homogeneity. On this basis it will be possible to assign relative ranks to groups of central places identified on the dendrogram. In the case of centres within a metropolitan region a centre which is composed of higher grade business types would be ranked above a centre composed of lower grade business types. In the case of central places within a rural region, when quality differences are not considered, a centre of greater complexity in terms of the variety and number of business firms would be regarded as the higher order centre. On this basis it is possible to grade the n groups of central places and thereby to classify each place.

As an example of an inter-urban hierarchy King's (1962) arrangement for Canterbury towns is shown in Fig. 4.4. The group A towns appear to have only relative size in common and show no strong tendency towards clustering. Of those in group B, King has found that only four (6, 7, 9, 10) group together satisfactorily and then only after the axes have been rotated and standard deviations used in place of the raw data (Fig. 4.7; for details of exact procedure see King, 1962). The boundary between groups B and C can only be determined arbitrarily and within group C further subdivision appears possible (King, 1962, p. 148).

Submitting King's data to the alternative analysis suggested in this chapter it is apparent in Fig. 4.10 that the dendrogram tends to confirm that the towns of group A (1, 2, 4, 3) show no strong tendency to cluster as the homogeneity between the four places of this single group vary from 0.75 to 0.61. In the case of group B towns only 5, 6, 7 and 9 show distinct association. All the remaining members of the group are more clearly associated with towns 8, 10, 11, 12, 13, . . ., 43, most of which occur in group C of Fig. 4.4.

The similarity between results obtained with the H'_{qm} function and its associated grouping procedure is further demonstrated with the aid of the data used in the Spokane and Snohomish county studies (Garrison *et al.*, 1959; Berry and Garrison, 1958a). In both instances it is possible to discern three major groups (Figs 4.11 and

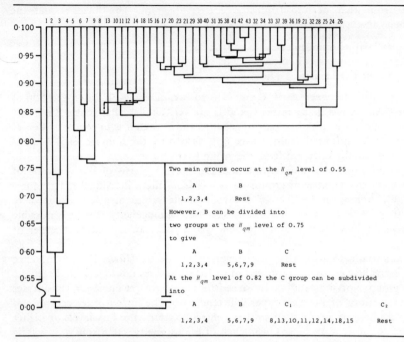

Fig. 4.10 Grouping of Canterbury towns on the basis of homogeneity values. Numbers along the upper axis correspond with the numbers in Fig. 4.4 (from Beavon, op. cit., 52, 1970b).

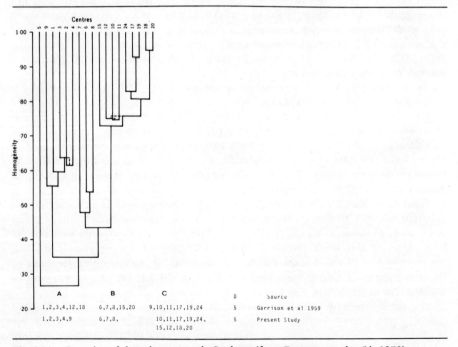

Fig. 4.11 Grouping of shopping centres in Spokane (from Beavon, op. cit., 54, 1972).

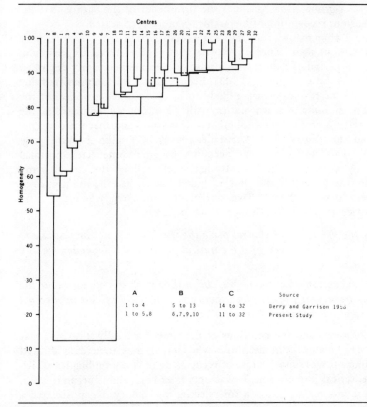

Fig. 4.12 Grouping of towns in Snohomish County. Numbers for different centres correspond with those of Fig. 2.1. Note that in the dendrograms (Fig. 4.11 and above) the letter C has been used to designate the lowest order group although in the scattergram of Berry and Garrison. (Fig. 2.1) the letter A has been used (from Beavon, op. cit., 54, 1972).

4.12) that correspond fairly closely with those already identified in the original studies. However, it would be possible to argue for the identification of still further groups within the C groups indicated. No attempt is made here to provide a set of 'rules' for determining breaks in the dendrogram. As stated in Chapter 2, similar sets of rules and the subjective application of a definition of a group appears to be contrived and might appear to be directed at establishing a hierarchy rather than for seeking a possible hierarchy. The use of logical argument in the interpretation of the dendrograms is favoured. Despite these remarks no attempt is being made in this chapter to show anything more than that the alternative procedure for identifying hierarchies, as here proposed, is at least comparable in the end result with those that have already been widely used. However, not only is a comparable end result produced but the taxonomic procedure does provide more information for interpretative purposes.

In this chapter attention has been drawn to the fact that hierarchies have been perhaps more readily recognised than has always been justified by the data. In some instances this has been due to a combination of the technique of classification that has been used and the fact that many geographers have subscribed to the Clark and

Evans definition of a group. However, it is the firm belief of the author that the reason for the persistent recognition of hierarchies is more deep-seated.

The point in time when many of the important studies cited in this chapter were undertaken is not without significance. In the late 1950s and early 1960s geography was emerging from a period of radical transformation that has been aptly described as the quantitative revolution (Burton, 1963). Even in 1963 Burton predicted that the consequences of the revolution were likely to involve the practitioners of the discipline in greater amounts of mathematics, with a concomitant emphasis on the construction and testing of mathematical models. It is significant that the quantitative revolution and the 'discovery' of Christaller's work by English-speaking geographers coincided. This in many ways accounts for the somewhat emotional statements made by Bunge, but statements that surely echoed the cry of many others at the time (the present author not excluded), when he rang the praises of Christaller and central place theory. Two statements, one already referred to in Chapter 2, will suffice as illustration (Bunge, 1962, p. 129):

If it were not for the existence of central place theory, it would not be possible to be so emphatic about the existence of a theoretical geography independent of any set of mother sciences.

With the possible exception of cartography, the author is of the opinion that the initial and growing beauty of central place theory is geography's finest intellectual product and puts Christaller in a place of great honour.

Given these statements and the emotions of the time it is hardly surprising that hierarchies were demarcated even by those who stated that their data showed evidence of continua. It was simply a case of recognising the only finding for which there was any theoretical justification. It was only later that doubts began to arise, but even then there was no justification for rejecting the theory that postulated a stepped hierarchy.

In the previous chapters of this book some doubt has been expressed about the validity of the theory of tertiary activity. However, to counterbalance these reservations it has been shown how Christaller can be reinterpreted to provide the basis for a stepped hierarchical system of central places in which both excess and normal profits are possible. Furthermore, by introducing the geotaxonomic measure of similarity in this chapter an alternative technique has been demonstrated that is capable of recognising a hierarchy from data relating to the internal composition of central places.

It was with these thoughts in mind that in 1970 a study was undertaken to examine the structural component of the system of intra-metropolitan shopping centres in Cape Town (Beavon, 1972). The results of that study led to the search for an alternative theoretical base for understanding the location and composition of central places, a theoretical base for a continuum in an intra-metropolitan system. For this reason the Cape Town study is presented in detail in the chapter that follows.

Notes

1. The problem of applying the family of techniques, of which the Clark and Evans (1954) nearest neighbour technique is representative, have been outlined by Cowie (1968). The

usefulness in geography of defining a group in terms of proximity to members in a set is well discussed by Johnston (1968a) who follows an initial suggestion by D. W. Goodall (1963). Grigg (1965) has defined a group in a similar way to that of Clark and Evans.

2. In practice each property is divided by the largest value in the property row to give resultant values ranging between zero and unity. The procedure is termed maximum normalisation and is discussed and justified in Brundrit (1972) and Beavon (1974c).

3. A computer program, HOMGN, has been written in Fortran and adapted for ease of running on an IBM 370 system using off-line magnetic disc storage to facilitate clustering of data sets in excess of eighty items.

Chapter 5

The structure of extra-CBD shopping centres in metropolitan Cape Town

Founded in 1652 as a victualling station for ships en route between Europe and the Far East, Cape Town has only been subject to positive planning controls since the latter half of this century. For 300 years physical urban development in general, and business development in particular has been controlled by the forces of the market mechanism. When planning control in the form of zoning was introduced for the metropolitan area c. 1955 all tertiary businesses that had developed to that time were recognised and preserved by the zoning (Joint Town Planning Committee, 1955, p. 72). By 1970 (when data for this chapter was collected) only a few small planned shopping centres[1] had appeared. Thus a clearly defined intra-urban hierarchy of extra-CBD shopping centres of the type both postulated by the theory of tertiary activity and empirically observed in other metropolitan areas might reasonably be expected to occur in metropolitan Cape Town.

In this chapter data relating to the shopping centres in metropolitan Cape Town will be examined to see whether the expected hierarchy exists. In undertaking the analysis the presence of physical blight in shopping centres will be taken into account. The examination of the data will be made by application of the H'_{qm} measure and the associated average member linkage algorithm outlined in the previous chapter.

Shopping centres in metropolitan Cape Town

With a population of approximately 1.1 million of which almost 379,000 are classified as White, metropolitan Cape Town (Fig. 5.1) is both the oldest and second largest urban area in South Africa. As in the case of Christchurch, and apparently in contradiction to cases reported in North America (W. A. V. Clark, 1967), shopping centres tend towards a linear rather than a nucleated form.

In this study of Cape Town a business centre is defined as a single business or an association of businesses each one of which is within at least 90 metres of another similar type of business[2]. A total of 643 extra-CBD centres with an aggregate of 5,805 businesses were delimited for study[3] (Fig. 5.2). The number of businesses per centre ranged from a single shop to 421 in the case of the largest centre, that of Parow (district 27, Fig. 5.1).

In South Africa there is a distinct tendency for medical and other professional practices, insurance and building society agencies as well as other services to be located in major business centres. The extent to which such activities are located in a particular centre is considered indicative of its overall centrality and relative hierarchical status. For this reason both office and service businesses have been

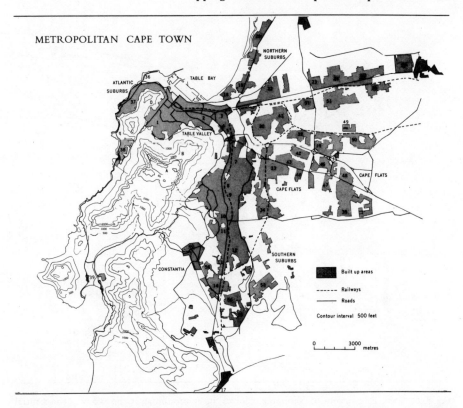

Fig. 5.1   Metropolitan Cape Town. Numbers refer to major districts as follows: 1 Central Cape Town, including the CBD; 2 Woodstock; 3 Salt River; 4 Observatory; 5 Mowbray; 6 Rosebank;   7 Rondebosch;   8 Newlands;   9 Claremont;   10 Kenilworth;   11 Wynberg; 12 Plumstead;   13 Dieprivier;   14 Bergvliet;   15 Muizenberg;   16 St. James;   17 Kalk Bay; 18 Paarden Eiland (Industrial Area); 19 Brooklyn; 20 Milnerton; 21 Maitland; 22 Windermere;   23 Goodwood;   24 Vasco;   25 Epping;   26 Elsiesrivier;   27 Parow;   28 Tiervlei; 29 Bellville;   30 Pinelands;   31 Epping Industrial;   32 Langa;   33 Athlone and Crawford; 34 Lansdowne;   35 Nyanga;   36 Green Point;   37 Sea Point;   38 Camps Bay;   39 Hout Bay; 40 Constantia; 41 Thornton; 42 Bridgetown; 43 Silvertown; 44 Rylands Estate; 45 Bonteheuvel;   46 Welcome Estate;   47 Surrey Estate;   48 Duinefontein;   49 Matroosfontein; 50 Bishop Lavis; 51 Kewtown; 52 Bothasig; 53 Grassy Park; 54 Retreat; 55 Steenberg; 56 Meadowridge; 57 Lakeside.

Letters refer to major topographical features as follows: A Table Mountain (3,566 ft); B Devil's Peak (3,284 ft); C Lions Head (2,196 ft); D Lion's Rump (part of Signal Hill, 1,153 ft) (from Beavon, op. cit., 54, 1972).

included in the analysis that follows. In the event of two centres being identical in terms of premises occupied it can happen that one centre contains vacant premises. It is felt that in such a case the two shopping centres cannot be equated overall, and such a difference should be taken into account when comparing centres one with another. For this reason the vacancy category is included in the business classification that is discussed below.

In order to denote the status of any business a grading of four classes of physical blight[4] has been employed (Table 5.1). As a result the final classification of

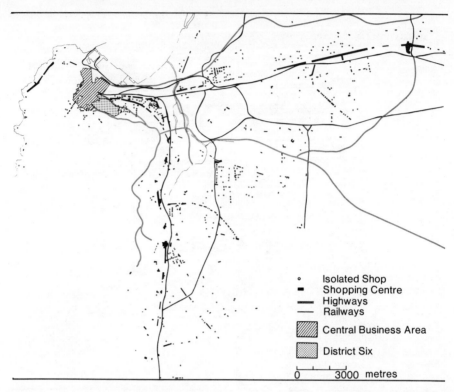

Isolated Shop
Shopping Centre
Highways
Railways

Central Business Area

District Six

0   3000 metres

Fig. 5.2   The distribution of shopping centres in metropolitan Cape Town. The central business area represents the CBD and Frame. At the time of the survey (1970) District Six was in a state of demolition with families being rehoused on the Cape Flats (Fig. 5.1) and was excluded from the survey (from Beavon, op. cit., 54, 1972).

business types recognised in the field consists of 142 categories (Table 5.2)[5]. For the purpose of the geotaxonomic analysis it has been necessary, because of technical limitations and storage capacity of available computer facilities[6], to limit the data matrix to 143 centres and 142 property rows. In reducing the original matrix of 643 centres and 142 property rows, 500 shopping centres of five businesses or less were excluded. The smallest centre thus included in the restricted data matrix of metropolitan shopping centres has six businesses.

Table 5.1   Criteria for grading single businesses (after Beavon, op. cit., 54, 1972).

Grade	Characteristics
A	Physical appearance superior to Grade B
B	Out-of-date shop-fittings, poor paintwork, cracked glassware
C	As in Grade B with the addition of deterioration in plaster and/or woodwork, ceilings, floors
D	Complete deterioration

Table 5.2 Classification and grading of business types observed in shopping centres of metropolitan Cape Town (after Beavon, op. cit., **54**, 1972).

Graded business cat. no.	Category	Ungraded business cat. no.
1—4	Café	1
5—8	General dealer	2
9—12	Fruiterer	3
13 15	Baker/Confectioner	4
16—18	Butcher	5
19—21	Fishmonger/Fish and chips shop	6
22	Delicatessen	7
23—25	Dairy	8
26—28	Grocer/Supermarket	9
29	Restaurant	10
30	Chain store (food dominant)	11
31—32	Chain store, clothing	12
33—36	Clothing, men	13
37—40	Clothing, women	14
41—44	General clothes	15
45—47	Clothing, children	16
48—50	Shoes	17
51—53	Drapers/Wool/Sewing shop	18
54—57	Bar/Bottle store	19
58—60	Furniture, new	20
61—63	Furniture, used	21
64—65	Household appliances	22
66—68	Hardware	23
69—71	Soft furnishers	24
72—74	Motor service and repairs	25
75—76	Motor sales, new	26
77—80	Motor sales, used	27
81—83	Cinema	28
84—86	Florist	29
87—89	Jeweller	30
90	Antiques	31
91—92	Gift shop	32
93—94	Bookshop/Stationer	33
95—97	Sports shop/Toy shop	34
98—99	Pharmacy	35
100—101	Variety/Departmental chain store	36
102—103	Variety/Departmental store (non-chain)	37
104—107	Other retailers	38
108	Bank	39
109	Bank agency	40
110	Insurance (only)	41
111	Building society (only)	42
112—114	Real estate/Insurance/Building society agency	43
115—118	Medical/Para-medical practioner	44
119—120	Other professional service	45
121—124	Clothing service	46
125—128	Household service	47
129—132	Barber/Beauty/Hair salon	48
133	Post Office	49
134	Library	50
135	Library, branch	51
136—138	Other service	52
139—142	Vacancy	53

Hierarchical analysis of the shopping centres

The metropolitan system

The application of the frequency modulated relative homogeneity measure, and the use of the calculated average member linkage algorithm to the largest possible matrix of 143 centres by 142 properties reveals comparatively little dendrographic structure between the 143 centres (Fig. 5.3). If it is assumed that there is a distinct similarity between the commercial structure of business centres outside the CBD in both South Africa and the United States, the dendrogram may suggest the possible existence of four groups at the 55 per cent level of homogeneity. In view of the uncertainty of this comparability (Beavon, 1970a) it is advisable to proceed with caution and to resist the expedient temptation to recognise a four-level extra-CBD hierarchy.

It is possible and necessary when using a dendrogram for the purpose of determining a hierarchy to compare individual members, or the average member of one group, with that of another and on this basis to assign a rank. The dendrogram merely shows the resemblance between individual members and groups of members; it does not in itself indicate the rank of a group. Notwithstanding, those members with a greater number of businesses and greater range of business types will *tend* to be the higher order centres and will be more heterogeneous than smaller centres. As such the link levels of higher order centres will tend to be at lower levels of homogeneity. Closer inspection of the centres in the possible groups A, B and C (Fig. 5.3) reveals their pattern of location. It is common knowledge that Wynberg and Claremont are the two major centres in the Southern Suburbs of Cape Town whereas Parow and Bellville occupy similar positions in the Northern Suburbs. The Sea Point centre is the major centre to the northwest of the CBD. The single member group B must be regarded as an intermediate case in that it is only slightly more similar to the Southern Suburbs group than it is to the centres of the Northern and Northwestern suburbs.

Intuitively it would appear unreasonable to assign different ranks to any of the three possible groups. On the basis of 143 centres grouped in terms of 142 properties it appears reasonable to argue that only two groups can be recognised, viz., (A, B, C) as one and (D) as the other. The latter group consists of 134 centres that show a relatively high degree of homogeneity across a large proportion of the constituent centres. In addition the incremental differences in homogeneity in each successive link is very small. The existence of only two groups, the one consisting of nine centres, the other of 134 centres with a predominance of single item linkages, provides little evidence for recognising a clear hierarchical structure of the type postulated by theory. It is concluded that across 94 per cent of the centres a continuum exists.

Elimination of differential blight

In order to test whether the lack of a readily distinguishable hierarchy among Cape Town shopping centres is attributable to the recorded presence of differential blight within and between centres it is necessary to eliminate this effect. In so doing the number of property rows in the data matrix is reduced from 142 to 53 (Table 5.2). Analysis of the original 143 centres on this basis yields the taxonomic grouping shown in Fig. 5.4.

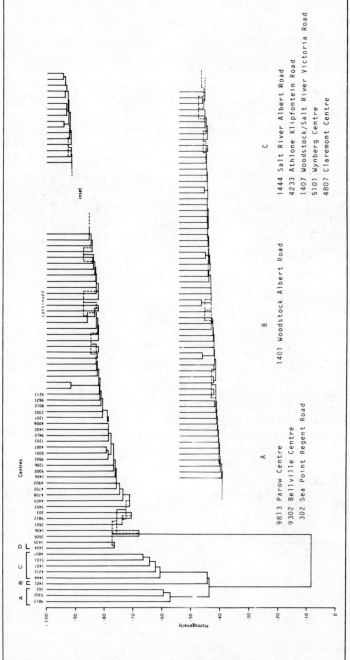

Fig. 5.3 Grouping of 143 business centres on the basis of 142 categories of business (see Table 5.2) (from Beavon, op. cit, 54, 1972).

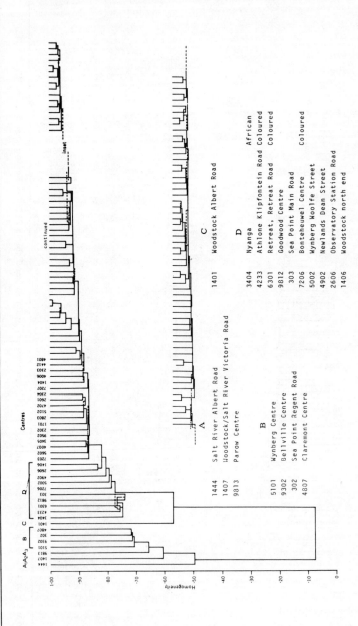

Table 5.4 Grouping of 143 business centres after the exclusion of differential blight has reduced the number of business categories to 53 (see Table 5.2) (from Beavon, op. cit., **54**, 1972).

Whereas this dendrogram is similar to that based on 142 properties (Fig. 5.3), a greater amount of structure is discernible. Group B (Fig. 5.4) consisting of four members, Wynberg Centre, Bellville Centre, Sea Point Main Road, and Claremont Centre, shows a 70 per cent homogeneity. Three individual members, Salt River Lower Main Road (A_1), Salt River Victoria Road (A_2), and Parow Centre (A_3), link successively to group B, and the seven centres (i.e., A_1, A_2, A_3, and group B) could possibly be considered as a first-order group. The single group constituted by Woodstock Albert Road (C) is again an intermediate case. A possible second order group (D), consisting of important business centres, one African, three Coloured, and six White, shows signs of a break between the remainder of the centres.

From the structure of the dendrogram it would appear that at least some basis for hierarchical grouping has been provided through a reduction in the number of property rows of the data matrix (cf. Figs 5.3 and 5.4). Nevertheless, it again appears that a case can be argued for a continuum over approximately 94 per cent of the centres.

Shopping centres in the White areas

The warning has been given by Marshall (1969) that a continuum might well result when centres are analysed without due regard to their geographical locations. Whereas this would appear to be a sound warning when dealing with central places as part of a system of towns in a regional setting, it would appear less pertinent when considering business centres within a city. Up to the present the literature claims that no difficulty has been encountered in recognising hierarchies of intra-urban business centres (as pointed out in Chapter 2). The commercial areas of Cape Town radiate outwards along good transportation links that make the CBD very accessible (cf. Figs 5.1 and 5.2). There appears to be little reason for doubting that the business centres of metropolitan Cape Town are not members of a single system. However, given the separation of residential areas for different racial groups it can be argued that business centres serving a predominantly Coloured clientele[7] constitute a system separate from the remainder.

Accepting that a case might exist for distinguishing between Coloured and White business centres, a data matrix has been compiled consisting of 143 White business centres containing 134 of the 142 business types graded according to the incidence of blight (Table 5.2). Included in the 143 White centres[8] are Parow with 421 businesses and single corner store 'centres'. *Dendrographically* (Fig. 5.5) the results of the analysis are similar to those already discussed. It would be reasonable to recognise nine centres as a possible first order group in which A_1, A_2, and A_3 can perhaps be distinguished from the five centres indicated as group (B). Once again centre 1401, Woodstock Albert Road, as well as centre 1404 at the north end of Albert Road appear as an intermediate order. However, over the remaining 133 centres, i.e., 94 per cent of the set, a continuum exists as indicated by a predominance of single item linkage and small incremental steps. Therefore it appears that not only is there a continuum of shopping centres in metropolitan Cape Town (Fig. 5.3) but also a continuum for the set of shopping centres located in the predominantly White areas of the city. If for the White shopping centres the existence of differential blight is ignored, then the data matrix again reduces to one of 143 business centres and 53 property rows. The results of this analysis are given in the dendrogram presented in Fig. 5.6. Apart from a tighter grouping exhibited in the group of centres (A) the group of centres (B) can be distinguished from what might

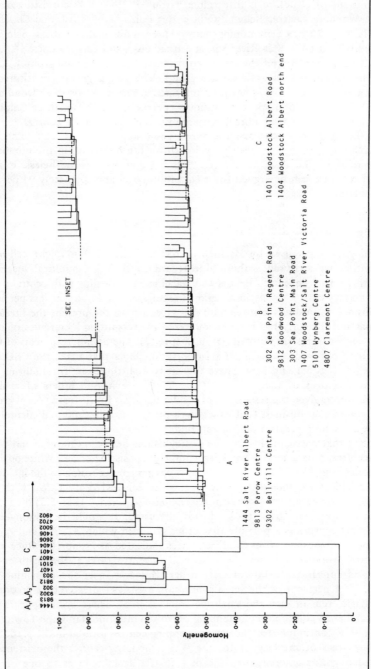

Fig. 5.5   Grouping of 143 business centres, located in predominantly White areas, on the basis of 142 business categories.

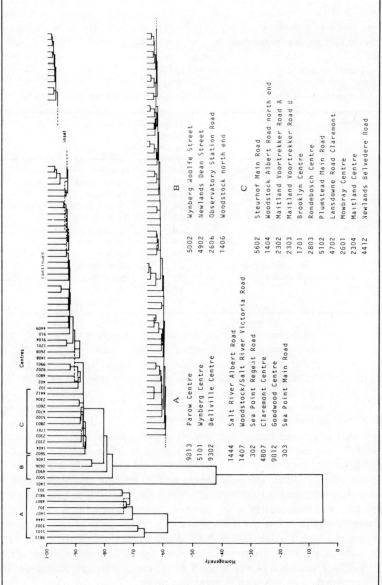

Fig. 5.6 Grouping of 143 White business centres, ignoring the existence of differential blight (from Beavon, op. cit., 54, 1972).

be termed a third order group (C). Yet again centre 1401 appears as an intermediate centre between groups (A) and (B).

Reduction of the business categories

As it appears that the elimination of grades of blight *and* the separation of Coloured from White business centres together contribute to greater hierarchical structuring, two further analyses are suggested. In the first instance the fifty-three business types used are regrouped into twenty-four types by combining several individual categories into a single collective category (Table 5.3). Using the same 143 White

Table 5.3   A restricted classification of business types (after Beavon, op. cit., 54, 1972).

Ungraded business cat. no.	Category	Ungraded business cat. no.	Category
1	Café/General dealer	13	Jeweller
2	Fruiterer	14	Gifts, books, toys, sports
3	Baker/Confectioner	15	Pharmacy
4	Butcher	16	Variety and department stores
5	Fishmonger/Fish and chips	17	Banking
6	Dairy	18	Insurance and finance
7	Grocer/Supermarket/Delicatessen	19	Professional service
8	Clothing and drapers	20	Clothing and household services
9	Furniture/Household appliances	21	Other services
10	Motor sales and service	22	Post Office
11	Cinema	23	Libraries
12	Florist	24	Bottle store/Bar

centres the analysis is repeated and the dendrogram is shown in Fig. 5.7. In this instance considerably more group structure is seen than has been the case previously. A first order group with the clearest subdivision yet is shown in A_1 and A_2. A second order group is readily discernible. Once again it would be tempting to accept this particular classification as both meaningful and significant. The use of only a rather unrealistic twenty-four business types in the data matrix argues against such an acceptance. It also suggests that whereas the reduction in the property rows has assisted in promoting a possible hierarchical structure a similar result could be obtained by a less drastic and more reasonable reduction and merging of business types. To test this assertion a final data matrix was prepared in which class differences were again eliminated and several business types considered to be those that distinguished the highest order extra-CBD White business centres from the other business centres were grouped together. In addition the vacancy category was disregarded. The net result was a data matrix of the 143 White centres and thirty-nine property rows (Table 5.4). Analysis of this matrix confirms the supposition that a reasonable reduction of the original fifty-three business types produces readily discernible groups (Fig. 5.8). These groups are similar to those obtained from the data matrix with twenty-four property rows (Fig. 5.7).

Recognition of a continuum

It is clear from the material presented above that a continuum of shopping centres in metropolitan Cape Town occurs except where the effects of differential blight

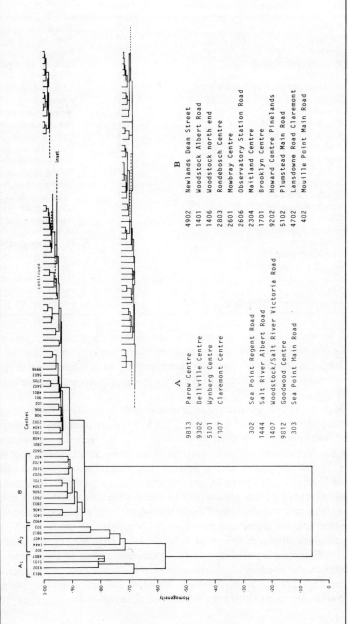

Fig. 5.7 Grouping of 143 White business centres on the basis of only 24 generalised business categories (see Table 5.3) (from Beavon, op. cit., 54, 1972).

Table 5.4   An alternative classification of business types (after Beavon, op. cit., 54, 1972).

Ungraded business cat. no.	Category	Ungraded business cat. no.	Category
1	Café	16	Bar/Bottle store
2	General dealer	17	Furniture, new
3	Fruiterer	18	Furniture, used
4	Baker/Confectioner	19	Household appliances
5	Butcher	20	Hardware
6	Fishmonger/Fish and chips	21	Soft furnishers
	Delicatessen	22	Motor service and repair
	Restaurant	23	Motor sales, new
	Chain store, food	24	Motor sales, used
	Chain store, clothing	25	Other cinema
7	Variety and department store	26	Other florist
	Antiques	27	Other Jeweller
	Gifts	28	Books and stationery
	Luxury cinema	29	Sports and toys
	Grade A florist	30	Pharmacy
	Grade A jeweller	31	Other retail
8	Dairy	32	Banking
9	Grocer/Supermarket	33	Insurance and finance
10	Clothing, men	34	Professional service
11	Clothing, women	35	Clothing service
12	General clothes	36	Household service
13	Clothing, children	37	Barber/Beauty/Hair salon
14	Shoes	38	Public service
15	Draper/Wool/Sewing shop	39	Other service

within and between centres is ignored. Clearer hierarchical groups become apparent by ignoring the existence of blight and by successively combining the original business categories into few categories. However, any clear hierarchical division that can be discerned from the analysis of the reduced data matrices must be regarded as contrived[9].

It has been suggested by Berry and Barnum (1962, p. 46) in their Iowan study that at the aggregative level of a central place system the blending of many varying but locally homogeneous subsystems leads to the emergence of a continuum of central places. Yet under such circumstances no attempt was made to accept the continuum as the *de facto* description of the central place system. Instead a hierarchy of the type postulated by central place theory, and the theory of tertiary activity, was accepted as the description of the system, despite the fact that such a hierarchy would only be recognised once the aggregative effects of the continuum had been extracted (see Berry and Barnum, 1962, p. 67).

By mapping the different orders of central places indicated on the dendrograms (Figs 5.3 to 5.8) the aggregative effects of the continuum can be overcome. This has been undertaken and the spatial distribution of different orders of central places are indicated in Figs 5.9 to 5.14. However, there is still no basis for recognising a stepped hierarchy no matter how regular the spatial distribution may appear to be.

A study of the structural components of shopping centres in metropolitan Cape Town has been presented in this chapter. The data matrix did not include as a parameter the population served by particular shopping centres. It did, however, include observations of the presence of physical blight. Furthermore the classifica-

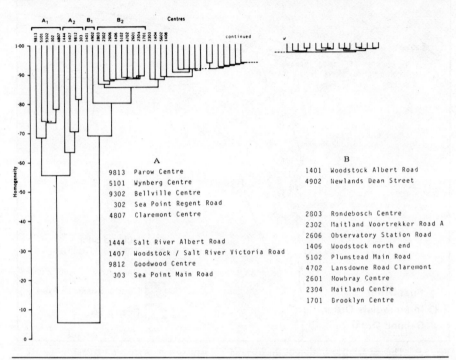

Fig. 5.8   Grouping of 143 White business centres on the basis of 39 generalised business categories (see Table 5.4) (from Beavon, op. cit., **54**, 1972).

tory approach adopted here made use of a technique developed from numerical taxonomy, a technique that has been shown to be capable of identifying fairly clear-cut hierarchies as identified elsewhere (cf. Chapter 4). Nevertheless, as now shown, the only logical conclusion that can be drawn is that when the full spectrum of shopping facilities and types is included in the data matrix there appears to be no basis for recognising a hierarchy. Particularly not a hierarchy of the kind postulated by either classical central place theory or the theory of tertiary activity.

While not gainsaying the usefulness of a hierarchical framework for the analysis of urban systems, it appears from the above study and the evidence presented in Chapter 4 that there is a need for exploring the possibility of providing a theoretical base for the observed continua. If such a base is provided then the hierarchical concept *as the basis for relative ranking* of central places is in no way invalidated. However, the inference that any place of a particular order contains *inter alia* all the activities of a lower order central place *and* is clearly differentiated would be invalidated. The provision of a theoretical base for the observed continuum of central places is a logical necessity. The work of both Christaller and Berry and Garrison fails to provide theoretical support for a continuum, as opposed to a stepped hierarchy, of intra-urban central places. An alternative theory is required. The key to such an alternative can be found in the work of August Lösch. That it has not been found hitherto is due to the difficulty urban geographers have had replicating Lösch's derivation of market areas. Until recently no complete derivation existed in the literature. The *a priori* derivation of the Löschian system of

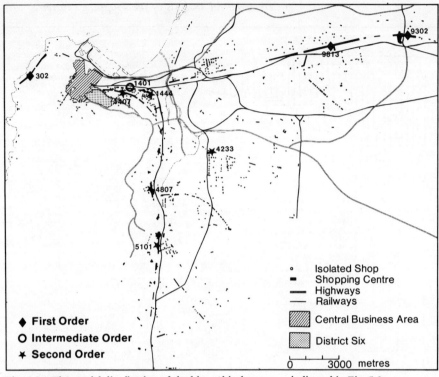

Fig. 5.9 The spatial distribution of the hierarchical structure indicated in Fig. 5.3.

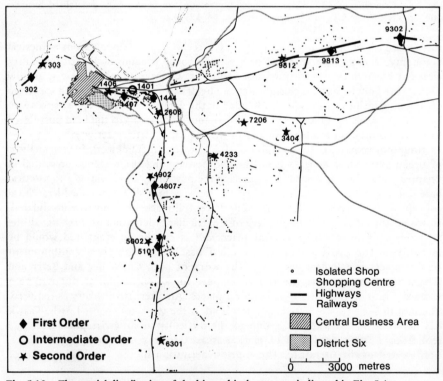

Fig. 5.10 The spatial distribution of the hierarchical structure indicated in Fig. 5.4.

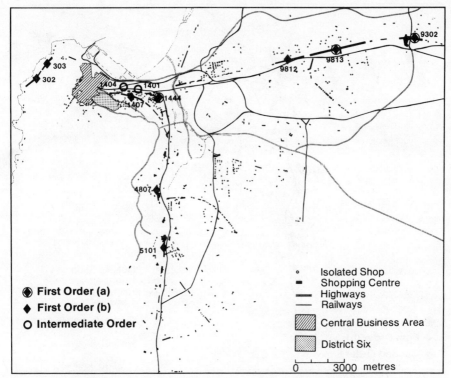

Fig. 5.11 The spatial distribution of the hierarchical structure indicated in Fig. 5.5.

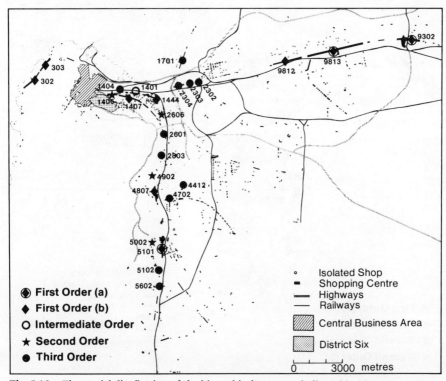

Fig. 5.12 The spatial distribution of the hierarchical structure indicated in Fig. 5.6.

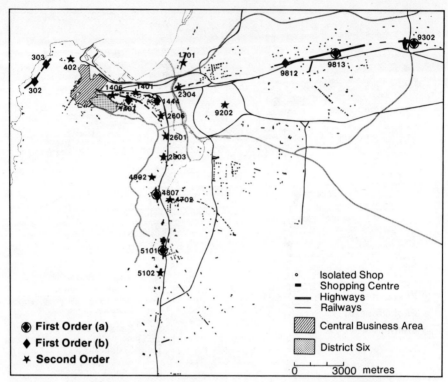

Fig. 5.13 The spatial distribution of the hierarchical structure indicated in Fig. 5.7.

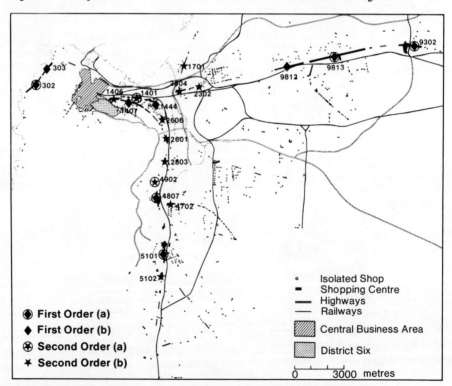

Fig. 5.14 The spatial distribution of the hierarchical structure indicated in Fig. 5.8.

market areas will be presented in Chapter 6. It will then be shown, in the chapters that follow, how it is possible to extend the ideas of Lösch and blend them with ideas from the work of Christaller and Berry and Garrison to develop an alternative theory of the location of intra-metropolitan tertiary activity.

Notes

1. This applies only to the free-standing shopping centres. Small planned developments within established shopping centres are naturally regarded as part of that shopping centre.
2. In the Cedar Rapids study (Garrison *et al.*, 1959) and in the Christchurch study (Clark, W. A. V., 1967), the distance separating two centres was taken as 61 m (200 ft), whereas in the study of southwestern Iowa (Berry *et al.*, 1962) the critical interval was 91 m (300 ft).
3. Both the delimitation of shopping centres outside the CBD and the classification of the businesses were made in the field by the author.
4. Based on the classification of Berry, 1963.
5. In practice not all classes of business were applicable to each category. For example, a class D dairy would not be permitted to operate under the public health regulations.
6. Initially an IBM 360/50 and only later an IBM 370/145.
7. The same argument is not applied to African shopping centres as only one of any significance occurred in the study area. It was removed from the data matrix in the ensuing analyses.
8. The 143 White centres includes 85 centres from the original matrix of 143 centres of all parts of the metropolis. To the 85 White centres a further 58 White centres, selected at random from the set of White centres not yet analysed and including 5 businesses or less, were added.
9. Making use of two suites of agglomerative polythetic classification programs Walmsley (1974) has recently concluded that no definite hierarchy of the type postulated by central place theory exists in southwest Sydney.

Chapter 6

Re-examination of the Löschian system of market areas

In the year following the translation and publication of August Lösch's *Die räumliche Ordnung der Wirtschaft* as *The Economics of Location*, Wolfgang Stolper (1955), one of the translators, made the comment that the Löschian system of market areas may refer as readily to tertiary activity as to secondary activity. Stolper, although probably the first to recognise the possibility of interpreting Lösch on an intra-urban scale, is not the only person to have made this comment. Among others who have made the suggestion are Dacey (1965b), Haggett (1965), Yeates and Garner (1971), Lloyd and Dicken (1972), Parr (1973), and most recently Bell *et al.* (1974). It appears that the stylised representation of Lösch's city-rich and city-poor landscape (Fig. 6.1) as presented by Haggett (1965) has been instrumental in encouraging the belief that the pattern of central places in the Löschian system appears to be in closer accord with reality than that of Christaller (Fig. 6.2). The Löschian system yields a more continuous distribution of central places than the step-like arrangement of the Christaller (and Berry and Garrison) hierarchy. In attempting to develop an intra-urban model that takes account of the intra-urban continuum of shopping centres, such as found in Cape Town, the challenge of re-examining Lösch's work cannot be ignored.

Among some who have expressed the belief that the Löschian system is more attractive than that of Christaller, the interpretation of the functional hierarchy of the Löschian system has been based solely on the *number* of activities found at a place without due allowance being made for the fact that the activities themselves may be different (e.g., Haggett, 1965; Yeates and Garner, 1971; Lloyd and Dicken, 1972). It appears that the lack of attention given to Lösch's work, and the relatively low level of interpretation thereof, is due in part to the greater complexity of the Löschian model (Hurst, 1972, p. 204). Indeed, it is only through a clear understanding of exactly *how* the Lösch network of markets and system of networks is derived that it becomes possible to interpret the Lösch system on an intra-urban scale, and to provide an alternative model of the location of intra-metropolitan tertiary activity.

Whereas the work of Lösch was rejected in 1958 by geographers (Berry and Garrison, 1958c) it has remained topical among economists and econometricians. A fierce debate has raged over whether a hexagonal or circular market area allows for maximum profits. Mills and Lav (1964) determined that Lösch (1954), and thereafter Valavanis (1955), and Kuenne (1963) were all incorrect in assuming that a necessary condition for equilibrium with profit maximisation is that market areas be space filling and hence hexagonal. The Mills—Lav findings, presented as a theorem, certainly threw doubt on the validity of the Lösch system and this doubt carried over into geographical literature (Berry, 1967), thereby possibly reinforcing

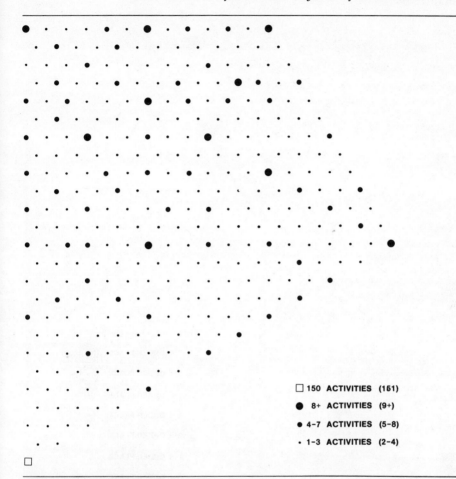

□ 150 **ACTIVITIES** (151)

● 8+ **ACTIVITIES** (9+)

● 4-7 **ACTIVITIES** (5-8)

· 1-3 **ACTIVITIES** (2-4)

Fig. 6.1 A 60 degree sector of the Löschian landscape. As each place is the centre of a basic activity the number of activities possessed by a place is as indicated in parentheses in the key. However, the more usual interpretation is as indicated on the left side of the parentheses (after Haggett, *Locational Analysis in Human Geography*, 1965).

the rejection of the Lösch system of central places. However, as indicated by Hartwick (1973) a conjecture that the Mills—Lav analysis is marred by an error[1] was mooted in 1970 by Denike and Parr (1970). Furthermore, independent studies by Beckmann (1970), Greenhut (1970), Hartwick (1970, 1973), Bollabas and Stern (1972), Stern (1972), and Greenhut and Ohta (1972) have all isolated the Mills— Lav error. In so doing the fundamentally important assumption of Greenhut (1970, p. 311) that the hexagon is the only competitive stable equilibrium market area shape has been shown to be valid. The discussion that follows accepts this point.

Notwithstanding the all but passing attention paid to it by geographers the work of Lösch is generally held in high esteem: 'As with *The Theory of Games*, or Keynes' *General Theory*, the main ideas are few and appear utterly simple once popularised. They are *fortunate* ideas, that is, they have many consequences that matter and that are not obvious' (Valavanis, 1955). Despite this eloquent sentiment it appears that there are certain aspects of Lösch's classic work on the network of

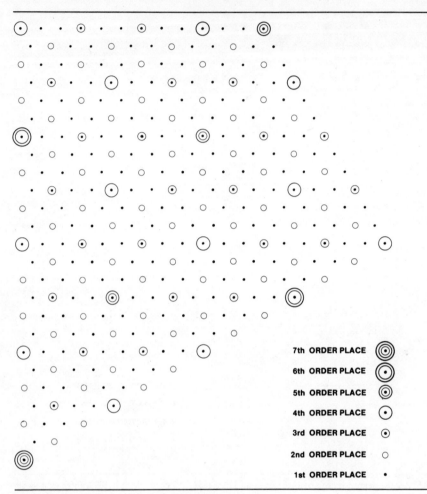

Fig. 6.2   A 60 degree sector of the Christaller K3 landscape.

markets and the system of networks that have not yet been clearly explained in the literature. Lösch himself does not describe his procedures of derivation in full and printing errors in certain equations that appear in the later translated text (1954) only serve to confuse the issue.

Statements outlining both the geometry of the Löschian system and the comparative geometry of his system and the Christallerian central place system have been published (Dacey, 1965a, b; Dacey and Sen, 1968; Hudson, 1967). Essentially, however, as Dacey has stated, these discussions have merely served to 'emphasise the geometric relations of a central place system. There is no attempt to develop the Christaller and Lösch systems from basic principles' (Dacey, 1965b, p. 111). Certainly five to eight years after the papers referred to on the geometry of the system were published, details on *how* the Löschian model is constructed remain minimal. In a selection of recent texts (Carter, 1972; Haggett, 1972; Lloyd and Dicken, 1972; Yeates and Garner, 1971) barely more than two or three pages in total are devoted to the work of Lösch. Whereas several of his well-known diagrams are reproduced no explanation of how they are constructed is offered. The derivation of the Lösch system should provide the necessary clarity.

A recent paper (Tarrant, 1973) has endeavoured to show how it is possible to develop the 'Löschian central place landscape' on a rhombic lattice using non-orthogonal reference axes. Unfortunately Tarrant considers only thirty-six of the 151 different sized hexagonal areas that go to make up the original Lösch system. Furthermore there is perhaps a misinterpretation of what was really meant by Lösch when he refers to rotation of the superimposed networks so that 'the greatest number of locations coincide' (Lösch, 1954, p. 124). It is only by generating the full Löschian scheme of regional centres that clarity on the above-quoted statement by Lösch can be obtained.

In this chapter an attempt will be made to show how the Löschian network of markets and system of networks can be deduced *a priori* using elementary co-ordinate geometry and a set of orthogonal reference axes. Secondly it will be shown how the deductions so made relate to the empirical equations supplied by Kanzig (Lösch, 1954, fn. 13a, p. 118) and Valavanis (1955). Furthermore, by generating the complete system of regional centres from 151 discrete networks of hexagonal markets it will be shown what is implied by Lösch's statement that the coincidence of centres be maximised.

Derivation of the size of markets

Having shown that a continuous system of markets in equilibrium would be composed of hexagonal market or trade areas for a region in which there was a continuous distribution of population (Lösch, 1954, pp. 110–14), Lösch then considered the nature of trade areas for an even but discrete distribution of population (Lösch, 1954, p. 114 *et seq.*). The basic settlement units, farmsteads, are assumed to be located on an isotropic surface to obviate irregular spatial variation. As all farms are of equal size a complete coverage of the plane with maximum density is possible if the farms take the shape of regular hexagons. The farmsteads are located at the centres of the farms. The resultant pattern of settlement must be a 60-degree lattice of places (farmsteads) separated from their nearest neighbours by a unit distance *a* (Fig. 6.3). This lattice will be referred to as the *basic lattice*.

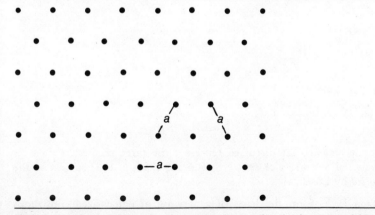

Fig. 6.3   The basic lattice. The distance between each pair of nearest neighbouring places is *a*.

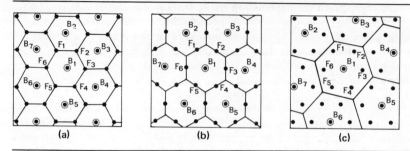

Fig. 6.4 The role of B towns. Each B town provides a portion of the services and commodities required by the surrounding farms: (a) each F farm receives one-third of its supplies from a B town; (b) each farm receives one-half from a B town; (c) each farm is totally supplied by the B town (reprinted from 'The Lösch System of Market Areas: Derivation and Extension,' by K. S. O. Beavon and A. S. Mabin, *Geographical Analysis*, Vol. 7, No. 2 (April 1975), 131–51. Copyright © 1975 by the Ohio State University Press).

The central farmstead in each group of seven eventually becomes a small market town B_r where certain commodities are available that would be purchased by each of the six surrounding farmsteads ($F_1, \ldots, F_6$). It is possible to draw three different sized market areas that would allow the B_r towns to serve the six farmsteads either partially or completely (Fig. 6.4) while at the same time serving themselves. In each of these three circumstances the distance between the B_r towns can be designated as a distance b'. In each of the three cases the value of b' will be different and it increases as the number of complete farmsteads served increases. In Fig. 6.4a the towns $B_1, B_2, B_3, B_4, B_5, B_6, B_7$, all provide part of the services and commodities required by the farmsteads $F_1, F_2, F_3, F_4, F_5, F_6$. In effect each of the B_r towns provides a third of the services and commodities required by the F_r farmsteads. Similarly, in the second case (Fig. 6.4b) each of the seven B_r towns provides half the services for each of the six F_r farmsteads, and in Fig. 6.4c each of the B_r towns provides all the services for each of the farmsteads. By elementary co-ordinate geometry it is possible to calculate the distance b' between a B_r town and its nearest neighbouring B_r town. In each of the three specific cases so far discussed this can be the distance between a pair of towns B_1 and B_6.

In Fig. 6.4a

$$b' = a\sqrt{3}$$

whereas in Fig. 6.4b

$$b' = \sqrt{[a^2 + (a\sqrt{3})^2]}$$
$$= a\sqrt{4}$$

and similarly in Fig. 6.4c

$$b' = \sqrt{[(2a)^2 + (a\sqrt{3})^2]}$$
$$= a\sqrt{7}$$

The three trade areas so far discussed represent the three smallest trade areas that can be drawn about a *service centre* B_r (Lösch, 1954, p. 117) subject to the constraints *implied* by Lösch, viz.,

(a) each hexagon is to form the basis of a network of equal sized contiguous hexagons, and

(b) the centre of each hexagon in a network of hexagons must be located at a place in the basic lattice.

It is possible, in accordance with the constraints just listed, to draw different sized trade areas about B_r that will serve larger numbers of farmsteads, e.g., nine and twelve. However, just as it is not possible to draw hexagonal trade areas around B_r centres so that they would serve only five or eight complete farmsteads, so too it is impossible to draw hexagonal trade areas which will serve completely ten, eleven or fourteen farmsteads. Whereas Lösch did not give the formula from which it is possible to calculate the number (n) of places that could be served by a hexagonal trade area (Lösch, 1954, fn. 13a, p. 118) this can be derived as follows.

The value of n

As stated the distance between adjacent points in the *basic lattice* is a. The distance q between any point and its second nearest neighbour is $a\sqrt{3}$ (Fig. 6.5a). The distance b'' from any one point in the lattice to any other point is calculated by simple application of Pythagoras' theorem to a triangle of the type shown in Fig. 6.5b. The basic lattice of points can be arranged on a set of orthogonal axes so that side y is always capable of expression in units of $a\sqrt{3}$, and side x in units of a (Fig. 6.5).

Therefore

$$b'' = \sqrt{[(k(a\sqrt{3}))^2 + (la)^2]} \qquad (6.1)$$

where k and l represent the number of units of $a\sqrt{3}$ and a respectively. The distances between A and B and between C and D (Fig. 6.5b) are thus:

$$b'' = \sqrt{[(2a\sqrt{3})^2 + (1a)^2]}$$
$$= a\sqrt{(13)}$$

and

$$b'' = \sqrt{[(\tfrac{1}{2}a\sqrt{3})^2 + (\tfrac{1}{2}a)^2]}$$
$$= a$$

respectively.

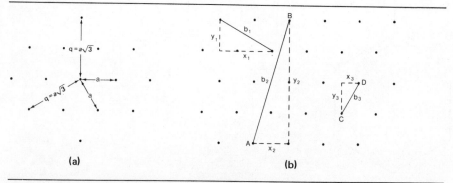

(a)   (b)

Fig. 6.5 Some distance relationships between places in the lattice. (a) Nearest and second nearest neighbour distances. (b) Distances b'' between any two points can be determined simply by use of the theorem of Pythagoras (reprinted from 'The Lösch System of Market Areas: Derivation and Extension,' by K. S. O. Beavon and A. S. Mabin, *Geographical Analysis*, Vol. 7, No. 2 (April 1975), 131–51. Copyright © 1975 by the Ohio State University Press).

Equation 6.1 becomes a more general expression when the values of k and l are allowed to vary to take account of all possible distances between an origin $(0, 0)$ and any point in a 30-degree sector of the lattice, now arranged on the orthogonal axes as described. That is when k assumes values of ½, 1, 1½, . . ., and $l = i + j$ where i assumes the value of ½ or 0 for alternate values of k, and j runs the integers 0 to $(k - i)$. The derivation presented so far accords with the empirical equations of Valavanis (1955).

For any planar shape the terms size and area are synonymous. Thus the size H of any regular hexagon with side s is given by

$$H = \frac{3s^2\sqrt{3}}{2} \qquad (6.2)$$

The distance b between the centres of any two regular hexagons with a common side s (Fig. 6.6) is given by

$$b = s\sqrt{3} \qquad (6.3)$$

Thus

$$s = b/\sqrt{3} \qquad (6.3.1)$$

substituting for s in equation 6.2 gives

$$H = \frac{b^2\sqrt{3}}{2} \qquad (6.4)$$

If *all* places (points) of the lattice (Fig. 6.3) are enclosed by regular hexagons (i.e., if the boundaries of Lösch's *farms* are drawn) the pattern appears as shown in

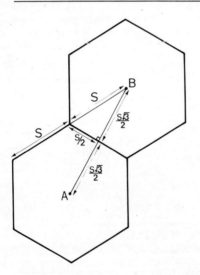

Fig. 6.6 Distance between the midpoints of any two contiguous regular hexagons with side s (reprinted from 'The Lösch System of Market Areas: Derivation and Extension,' by K. S. O. Beavon and A. S. Mabin, *Geographical Analysis*, Vol. 7, No. 2 (April 1975), 131–51. Copyright © 1975 by the Ohio State University Press).

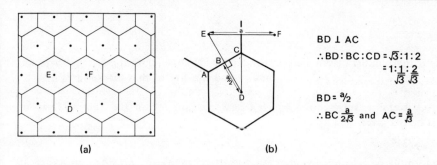

(a) (b)

Fig. 6.7 (a) The set of basic hexagons (H_0). (b) The sides of H_0 are $a\sqrt{3}$ (reprinted from 'The Lösch System of Market Areas: Derivation and Extension,' by K. S. O. Beavon and A. S. Mabin, *Geographical Analysis*, Vol. 7, No. 2 (April 1975), 131–51. Copyright © 1975 by the Ohio State University Press).

Fig. 6.7a and is sometimes described as the net of *basic hexagons* (Yeates and Garner, 1971). The side of these hexagons is $a/\sqrt{3}$ (Fig. 6.7b). Their size H_0 is obtained by substituting $a/\sqrt{3}$ for s in equation 6.2 to give

$$H_0 = \frac{a^2\sqrt{3}}{2} \tag{6.5}$$

The ratio n_r^* of any other hexagon of size H_r ($r = 0, 1, 2, 3, \ldots$) to the basic area H_0 is given by

$$n_r^* = H_r/H_0$$

whence

$$n_r^* = \left[\frac{b^2\sqrt{3}}{2}\right]\Big/\left[\frac{a^2\sqrt{3}}{2}\right]$$

and

$$n_r^* = b^2/a^2 \tag{6.6}$$

Let the distance a as defined above be unity. The distance b, in this case the distance between the centres of two hexagons H_r with a common side, can be calculated in exactly the same way as b'' from equation 6.1. The sum of $3k^2 + l^2$ for the successive pairs of values that can be assumed by k and l in equation 6.1 is always an integer. It follows therefore that the value of b^2 will always be an integer. Consequently n_r^* in equation 6.6 must always be an integer. A hexagonal market area of size H_0 encloses only one place in the lattice and it follows that the ratio n_r^* not only represents the relative areal size H_r of a hexagonal market area but the relative number of whole places enclosed by it. As such the n_r^* derived here is identical with the n termed by Lösch (1954, p. 119) the 'number of settlements completely supplied, including the point of supply; those partly supplied being reckoned in terms of the equivalent number of fully supplied settlements'.

It now follows that

$$b = a\sqrt{n_r^*} \tag{6.7}$$

and that[2]

$$H_r = \frac{a^2 n_r^* \sqrt{3}}{2} \qquad (6.8)$$

Thus if the number of supplied settlements n_r^* is known, both the distance between places that supply the same commodity and the size of that market area may be calculated.

If a is unity, substitution for b from equation 6.7 in the general form of equation 6.1 gives

$$n_r^* = (k\sqrt{3})^2 + l^2 \qquad (6.9)$$

The formula just deduced is identical with that empirically provided by Kanzig in the translated edition of Lösch (1954, p. 118).

An alternative procedure for calculating k and l

It is interesting to note that the procedure for calculating the values of k and l given by Kanzig (appearing on p. 119 of Lösch, 1954) is incorrect as published. Here a similar set of equations is presented in which, for the sake of comparison, Kanzig's notation is employed.

Let the index number, or subscript, of any hexagonal market area for which the number of settlements n is to be found be called h, where h can assume the integer values 0, 1, 2, 3, ... The problem is to find k and l for substitution in equation 6.9.

Having set h to zero first find an integer m such that

$$(m + 1)(m - 2) < h \leqslant (m + 1)(m - 2) + 2m \qquad (6.10)$$

Let

$$h_0 = (m + 1)(m - 2) + 2m \qquad (6.11)$$

Two cases now arise: if

$$(h_0 - h) < m \qquad (6.12)$$

then

$$k = \frac{2m - 1}{2} \qquad (6.13)$$

and

$$l = \frac{2m - 1}{2} - (h_0 - h) \qquad (6.14)$$

Alternatively, if

$$(h_0 - h) \geqslant m \qquad (6.15)$$

then

$$k = m - 1 \qquad (6.16)$$

and

$$l = (m - 1) - (h_0 - h) + m \qquad (6.17)$$

The value of n is now obtained from equation 6.9.

The nomenclature of area numbers

As n for a particular market area has been defined as n_r^* it follows that when the subscript h is set to zero the value of n_0^* for the basic hexagon of size H_0 can be obtained by following the procedure set out immediately above. Given that h is zero, k and l both assume values of ½, and n_0^* a value of 1. Following the same procedure it is possible to derive n_r^* for each hexagonal market area of size H_r for all integer values of r. For each assumed subscript number the procedure will define a particular value of k and l. It is therefore appropriate to indicate this by subscripting the symbols k and l hereafter. Among the possible values of the subscript r let any two be defined as α and β so that they are not equal. It is possible for a pair of values k_α, l_α and a pair k_β, l_β to give values of n_α^* and n_β^* that are identical. From equation 6.8 it will be seen that hexagons with size H_α and H_β will be identical although by definition $\alpha \neq \beta$.

As any two identical market areas on an isotropic plane can be expected to operate identically, Lösch was more concerned with distinguishing from among the set of hexagons with size H_r those that are not equal in size. To do this Lösch developed a nomenclature of *area numbers* A_p ($p = 0, 1, 2, 3, \ldots$) so that

$$A_0 < A_1 < A_2 < A_3 < \cdots < \cdots \tag{6.18}$$

Areas 1 to 9 (A_1 to A_9) are shown in Fig. 6.8.

The strict application of what are essentially the corrected Kanzig equations 6.10 to 6.17 followed by substitution in equation 6.9 will only produce the statistics for areas A_0 to A_{17} (Table 6.1), and up to this stage the index h is synonymous with the area number in accordance with inequality 6.18 (cf. Table 6.2). After the value of 17 the index h is no longer equal to the area number. By

Table 6.1 Unranked values of n^* derived from successive values of h and the associated values of m, k and l from equations 6.10 to 6.17 and 6.9 (reprinted from 'The Lösch System of Market Areas: Derivation and Extension,' by K. S. O. Beavon and A. S. Mabin, *Geographical Analysis*, Vol. 7, No. 2 (April 1975), 131–51. Copyright © 1975 by the Ohio State University Press).

h	n^*	k	l	m	h	n^*	k	l	m
0	1	½	½	1	19	48	4	0	5
1	3	1	0	2	20	49	4	1	5
2	4	1	1	2	21	52	4	2	5
3	7	1½	½	2	22	57	4	3	5
4	9	1½	1½	2	23	64	4	4	5
5	12	2	0	3	24	61	4½	½	5
6	13	2	1	3	25	63	4½	1½	5
7	16	2	2	3	26	67	4½	2½	5
8	19	2½	½	3	27	73	4½	3½	5
9	21	2½	1½	3	28	81	4½	4½	5
10	25	2½	2½	3	29	75	5	0	6
11	27	3	0	4	30	76	5	1	6
12	28	3	1	4	31	79	5	2	6
13	31	3	2	4	32	84	5	3	6
14	36	3	3	4	33	91	5	4	6
15	37	3½	½	4	34	100	5	5	6
16	39	3½	1½	4	35	91	5½	½	6
17	43	3½	2½	4	36	93	5½	1½	6
18	49	3½	3½	4	37	97	5½	2½	6

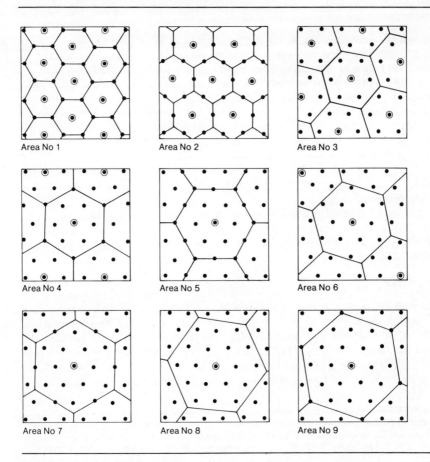

Fig. 6.8   The nine smallest areas of the Lösch system of market areas excluding A_0 (reprinted from 'The Lösch System of Market Areas: Derivation and Extension,' by K. S. O. Beavon and A. S. Mabin, *Geographical Analysis*, Vol. 7, No. 2 (April 1975), 131–51. Copyright © 1975 by the Ohio State University Press).

ranking the values of n_h^* ($h \geqslant 18$) the sequence of area numbers and their associated size and number of settlements served can be obtained. Where two different values of h give the same value of n_h^*, provision is made for the consideration of an alternative geometric arrangement of the hexagon for that particular area number. In Table 6.1 data is arranged for values of h from 0 to 37. Examination of the figures shows that for values of h equal to 18 and 20 the value of n_h^* is 49. Similarly, for values of h equal to 33 and 35 n_h^* is 91.

Ranking the data in Table 6.1 on the values of n_h^* and numbering the ranks successively from zero gives the area numbers of the Löschian system (Table 6.2). Naturally the pattern of values for k_h and l_h as previously shown in Table 6.1 is disrupted. For example, for A_{19} and A_{32} (Table 6.2) alternative sets of k_h and l_h (when $h = 20$ and $h = 35$ in Table 6.1) are shown that also yield values of 49 and 91 for n_{19}^* and n_{32}^* respectively [3].

Table 6.2 Area numbers based on the ranked values of n^* together with the associated values of k and l (reprinted from 'The Lösch System of Market Areas: Derivation and Extension,' by K. S. O. Beavon and A. S. Mabin, *Geographical Analysis*, Vol. 7, No. 2 (April 1975), 131—51. Copyright © 1975 by the Ohio State University Press).

Area no.	n^*	k	l	Area no.	n^*	k	l
0	1	½	½	19	49	3½	3½ or
1	3	1	0			4	1
2	4	1	1	20	52	4	2
3	7	1½	½	21	57	4	3
4	9	1½	1½	22	61	4½	½
5	12	2	0	23	63	4½	1½
6	13	2	1	24	64	4	4
7	16	2	2	25	67	4½	2½
8	19	2½	½	26	73	4½	3½
9	21	2½	1½	27	75	5	0
10	25	2½	2½	28	76	5	1
11	27	3	0	29	79	5	2
12	28	3	1	30	81	4½	4½
13	31	3	2	31	84	5	5
14	36	3	3	32	91	5	4 or
15	37	3½	½			5½	½
16	39	3½	1½	33	93	5½	1½
17	43	3½	2½	34	97	5½	2½
18	48	4	0	35	100	5	5

Derivation of the system of networks

If the exercise as shown in Table 6.1 is continued until the value of h is 183, sufficient data would be available to extend Table 6.2 to A_{150} as shown in Table 6.3. Just as it is possible to construct networks for A_0 to A_9 as illustrated in Fig. 6.8, so it is possible to construct networks for each of the 150 different sized areas. It is the superimposition of all 150 such networks that Lösch (1954, p. 124) refers to when he lays 'the nets so that *all* of them shall have at least *one* centre in common' from which his diagrams showing the location of regional centres and the coincidence of centres are respectively, partly, and wholly derived. For convenience the two diagrams are reproduced here as Figs 6.9 and 6.10 respectively.

Lösch stated that having laid the 150 nets upon each other so that they had at least one centre in common, they were rotated in order to produce six city-rich and six city-poor sectors with the greatest number of centres coinciding. It will be shown that Lösch achieved his results without actually physically resorting to either of the two procedures stated. This is primarily so because the production of city-rich and city-poor sectors is a *constraint* on the rotation rather than a consequence of it, an opinion that has also been expressed by Tarrant (1973). It will be shown that equations 6.9 to 6.17 provide the basis for locating the first centres away from the origin for the different networks — A_0 to A_{150} — and thereby the basis for locating all the centres that together produce the city-rich and city-poor sectors.

Whereas Lösch makes no explicit statement as to what he means by a city-rich sector, as opposed to a city-poor sector, a careful reading of his discussion on the general pattern of his system of networks (Lösch, 1954, pp. 124—6) makes it clear that he *implies* that a point in the lattice that serves as the coincident point for any

Table 6.3 The relationship between Area Number A_i and the number of effective customers n_i^*. Note that $n_0 = 1$ and $n_i = b_i^2$ (reprinted from 'The Lösch System of Market Areas: Derivation and Extension,' by K. S. O. Beavon and A. S. Mabin, *Geographical Analysis*, Vol. 7, No. 2 (April 1975), 131–51. Copyright © 1975 by the Ohio State University Press).

A_i	n_i^*	A_i	n_i^*	A_i	n_i^*	A_i	n_i^*	A_i	n_i^*
1	3	31	84	61	189	91	292	121	400
2	4	32	91	62	192	92	300	122	403
3	7	33	93	63	193	93	301	123	409
4	9	34	97	64	196	94	304	124	412
5	12	35	100	65	199	95	307	125	417
6	13	36	103	66	201	96	309	126	421
7	16	37	108	67	208	97	313	127	427
8	19	38	109	68	211	98	316	128	432
9	21	39	111	69	217	99	324	129	433
10	25	40	112	70	219	100	325	130	436
11	27	41	117	71	223	101	327	131	439
12	28	42	121	72	225	102	331	132	441
13	31	43	124	73	228	103	333	133	444
14	36	44	127	74	229	104	336	134	448
15	37	45	129	75	237	105	337	135	453
16	39	46	133	76	241	106	343	136	457
17	43	47	139	77	243	107	349	137	463
18	48	48	144	78	244	108	351	138	468
19	49	49	147	79	247	109	361	139	469
20	52	50	148	80	252	110	363	140	471
21	57	51	151	81	256	111	364	141	475
22	61	52	156	82	259	112	367	142	481
23	63	53	157	83	268	113	372	143	484
24	64	54	163	84	271	114	373	144	487
25	67	55	169	85	273	115	379	145	489
26	73	56	171	86	277	116	381	146	496
27	75	57	172	87	279	117	387	147	499
28	76	58	175	88	283	118	388	148	507
29	79	59	181	89	289	119	397	149	508
30	81	60	183	90	291	120	399	150	511

number of centres is a larger urban place than one at which a lesser number of centres are coincident. Consequently it must be expected that in the city-rich sector the number of places that are centres for 1, 2, 3, . . . coincidences of different centres of area ($A_0, A_1, A_2, A_3, \ldots$) will be greater than in the case of the city-poor sector.

It is appropriate at this stage to comment on the limits of a sector containing relatively many (city-rich) and relatively few centres (city-poor). This is necessary because Lösch failed to provide a clear description (Dacey, 1965b) but implies that the city-rich sector is larger in area than the city-poor sector. A study of his diagrams (Lösch, 1954, Figs 27 and 29) together with an analysis of the procedure employed for the construction of the diagram showing the location of regional centres (see Fig. 6.10), indicates that he included in his city-rich sector the places that lie *both on and between* the lines OY' and OC (Figs 6.11 and 6.12); whereas only those places *between* and *not on* the lines OC and OX' are included in the city-poor sector[4].

Lösch (1954, p. 124) correctly stated that with discontinuous settlement as represented by the basic lattice '*only* the networks of those market regions [areas] . . . lying obliquely can be rotated' (author's italics); e.g., Areas A_3, A_6, A_8, A_9, etc.,

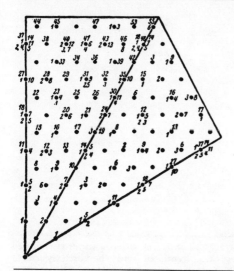

Fig. 6.9 The location of regional centres in a 60 degree sector: Lösch's original Figure 33 (from Lösch, *The Economics of Location*, 1954).

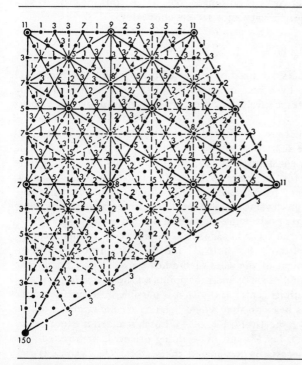

Fig. 6.10 The coincidence of centres of area in a 60 degree sector: Lösch's original Figure 32 (from Lösch, op. cit., 1954).

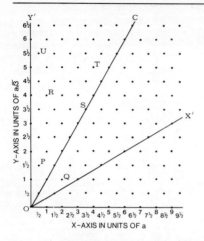

Fig. 6.11 The lattice of places arranged on orthogonal axes. The city-rich sector is indicated by $Y'OC$ and the city-poor sector lies *between* COX' (reprinted from 'The Lösch System of Market Areas: Derivation and Extension,' by K. S. O. Beavon and A. S. Mabin, *Geographical Analysis*, Vol. 7, No. 2 (April 1975), 131–51. Copyright © 1975, Ohio State University Press).

and not Areas A_1, A_2, A_4, etc. (Fig. 6.8). Furthermore, Lösch asserted that once network 3 (i.e., A_3) is located the choice of the relative position, implying *relative rotation*, of the remaining networks is no longer free. Indeed this must be so as a result of the self-imposed city-rich—city-poor sectors constraint.

Locating the centres of A_p ($p = 0, 1, 2, 3, \ldots$)

With the basic lattice of places arranged on a pair of orthogonal axes (Fig. 6.11) each place can be identified by a pair of co-ordinates (x, y) as indicated by the scales on the X- and Y-axes respectively. For the discussion that follows let a be set to unity.

The values of k_p and l_p that are substituted in equation 6.2 for A_p ($p = 0, 1, 2, \ldots, 35$) are shown in Table 6.2. Any pair of values for l_p and k_p represent the variables associated with the constants 1 and $\sqrt{3}$ in equation 6.9 and are therefore the (x, y) co-ordinate values for the centre of A_p. As the centres of all A_p ($p = 0, 1, 2, 3, \ldots$) areas can be arranged to coincide at the point $(0, 0)$ and as the distribution of all A_p centres for any given value of p will form a 60-degree lattice it is possible to derive all such locations after positioning the second A_p centre at (l_p, k_p).

The relative alignment of the basic hexagons A_0 is immaterial as their centres, the basic lattice of places, are fixed. For both A_1 and A_2 rotation would be meaningless as the resultant alignment of the sides of the hexagons can only remain the same in order to enclose a total of three and four points on the lattice respectively. In the case of A_3, located with its centre at $(0, 0)$, it is possible to select alternative alignments of the contiguous hexagon that would locate a *second centre* at either (½, 1½) or at (2, 1) (P and Q respectively, Fig. 6.11). Lösch selected the location of the second centre at (½, 1½), i.e., P, and in so doing oriented, or 'rotated', the whole A_3 network[5] and necessarily designated the sector $Y'OC$ as the city-rich sector to distinguish it from the sector between CO and OX'.

A perusal of Table 6.2 shows that there is only one location for the centre of the

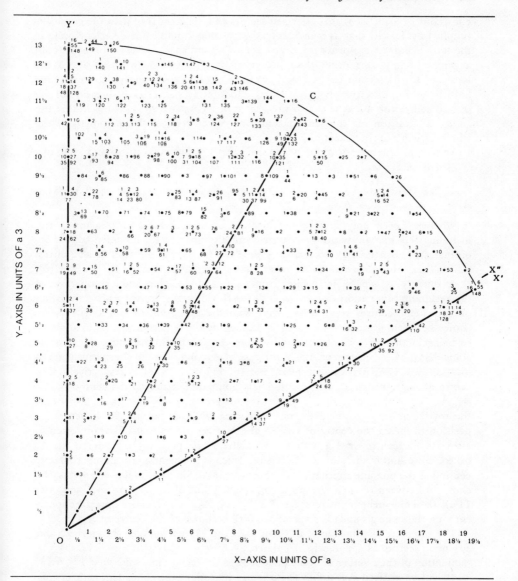

Fig. 6.12 The location of regional centres in the complete system. The numbers indicate that a place is a centre for A_p. All places are centres for A_0 and the origin is a centre for A_p ($p = 0, 1, 2, 3, \ldots, 150$) (reprinted from 'The Lösch System of Market Areas: Derivation and Extension,' by K. S. O. Beavon and A. S. Mabin, *Geographical Analysis*, Vol. 7, No. 2 (April 1975), 131–51. Copyright © 1975 by the Ohio State University Press).

second hexagon for each network up to and including A_{18} (given that it must fall within the city-rich sector $Y'OC$). In the case of A_{19} there are two sets of values (l_{18}, k_{18} and l_{20}, k_{20} in Table 6.1) that would give the location for the second centre of a hexagon in that network. Both a centre at $(1, 4)$ and $(3\frac{1}{2}, 3\frac{1}{2})$ would lie within the city-rich sector (R and S respectively, Fig. 6.11). Lösch selected the location $(3\frac{1}{2}, 3\frac{1}{2})$ i.e., S, as the second centre for A_{19}. This is in accordance with the constraint of areal inequality between sectors *and* in accordance with the condition (implied by Lösch) that as many centres as possible should coincide at any point in the lattice. Point S is already the centre for an A_0 and an A_3, whereas point R is not a centre of any area other than the common A_0. Area 32 has two alternative locations for its second centre: (4, 5) or (½, 5½) (T, U respectively, Fig. 6.11), and both lie within the city-rich sector. Lösch chose (4, 5), i.e., T, as the location of the second centre for A_{32} as it is also the centre of an A_0 and an A_3. In each case the choice of location for the second centre of A_p determines the alignment of the whole network of A_p hexagons.

Sets of alternative locations occur for twenty other areas up to and including A_{150}. They are:

A_{46}, A_{49}, A_{55}, A_{64}, A_{69}, A_{79}, A_{82}, A_{85}, A_{93}, A_{106}, A_{109}, A_{111}, A_{120}, A_{122}, A_{127}, A_{132}, A_{139}, A_{142}, A_{148}, A_{150}.

Whereas Lösch only showed the location of those centres of area up to and including A_{55} that lie within a city-rich and city-poor sector bounded by the co-ordinates (0, 0), (0, 6½), (6½, 6½), (9½, 3½), (9, 3), the location of all centres, other than those listed above that have alternative locations, is fixed[6]. Consequently, it is possible to infer from a series of trial plots and a comparison of the resultant summation of centres with Lösch's diagram, showing his summation of coincident centres (Fig. 6.10), that with the exception of A_{85} and A_{120} the choice between alternative locations is decided by the requirement that in addition to being in the city-rich sector the location chosen should maximise the possible coincidence of the centres of A_p. In the case of A_{85} and A_{120} the alternative pairs of locations are (7½, 8½) or (1½, 9½), and (6, 11) or (1½, 11½) respectively. The centre of A_{85} can therefore be located at a point that is already the centre for A_0, A_1, A_3, A_6 or at a point that is the centre for areas A_0, A_1, A_6, A_9. In either case the total number of coincident centres of area will then become 5. However, the decision to locate the centre of area 85 at (1½, 9½) *implies* that Lösch preferred to associate the centre of A_{85} with an A_9 centre as he probably considered the A_9 centre more important than an A_6 centre, which is the highest area number already centred at the possible alternative[7] point (7½, 8½). Similarly in the case of A_{120} the choice is between (6, 11), already a coincident point of A_0, A_1, A_3, A_8, and (1½, 11½), the coincident point of areas A_0, A_1, A_3, A_{21}. Lösch chose the latter apparently on the same grounds as given above for his choice of the centre of A_{85}.

The complete distribution of the centres of the 151 networks in the city-rich and city-poor sectors as apparently calculated by Lösch is shown in Fig. 6.12 and the summation of the number of coincident centres for each point is shown in Fig. 6.13.

It will be noticed that unlike the original diagram of the coincident centres (Fig. 6.9) showing two triangular areas, that presented here (Fig. 6.12) shows a 60-degree sector. The radius is the distance from the origin to the second centre of A_{150}. The summation of coincident centres[8] within the city-rich and city-poor sectors consequently represents only centres of areas A_1 to A_{150}. In his original diagram Lösch showed two 30-degree triangles bounded by the co-ordinates (0, 0), (0, 12), (12, 12), (18, 6). Such a boundary *includes* the centres of areas A_{151} at (9, 12), A_{156} at (10, 12), A_{161} at (11, 12), A_{166} at (12, 12), and A_{155} at (11½, 11½)[9]. *Excluded* are centres of areas A_{148} at (0, 13), A_{149} at (1, 13), A_{140} at (1½, 12½), A_{141} at (2½, 12½), A_{145} at (4½, 12½), A_{147} at (5½, 12½), and A_{150} itself at (2, 13).

A portion of a hexagon as used by Lösch (Fig. 6.9) might be appropriate when the inquiry is directed at the number and type of centres that are nested within the

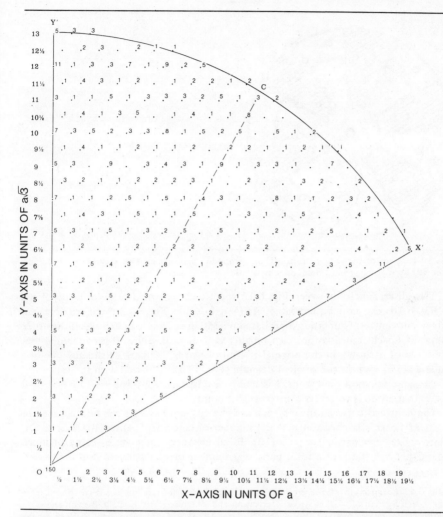

Fig. 6.13 The number of coincident centres for each point up to and including the second centre of A_{150} (reprinted from 'The Lösch System of Market Areas: Derivation and Extension,' by K. S. O. Beavon and A. S. Mabin, *Geographical Analysis*, Vol. 7, No. 2 (April 1975), 131–51. Copyright © 1975 by the Ohio State University Press).

boundary of a larger area. However, when the inquiry is directed at the number of coincident centres resulting from the theoretical superimposition of 150 (or N) discrete networks it appears more reasonable to use as a boundary an arc of a circle with centre $(0, 0)$ that will include, apart from the centre of A_{150} (or A_N) at the origin, the centre of A_{150} that is nearest to it. Alternatively it may be argued that a boundary which includes the centre A_{149} (or A_{N-1}) be used and the centre for A_{150} (or A_N) be represented at the origin only. In either case such a boundary appears more reasonable for the present purpose than that shown by Lösch that may exclude the centre of A_N and include centres of $A_{N'}$ $(N' > N)$, and it accords with his circular economic landscapes as shown in the first four diagrams of his chapter on the system of networks (e.g., see Fig. 6.14).

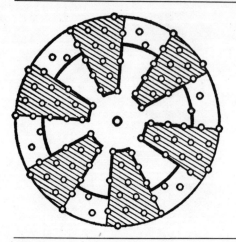

Fig. 6.14   The theoretical pattern of an economic landscape. The city-rich sectors are indicated by shading (from Lösch, op. cit., 1954).

Two discrepancies between Fig. 6.12 and Lösch's original diagram (reproduced as Fig. 6.10) can now be indicated. At (4½, 11½) on Fig. 6.12 there are only *two* coincident centres. Numerous trials based on 150 areas, while matching all the other values of Lösch, failed to produce a higher value for this point. It is concluded that the value of 7 shown in the original is a misprint for 2. Likewise the absence of a value at (5½, 9½) on the original diagram (Fig. 6.10) compared with the value of 1 at the same location on Fig. 6.13 is due to a misprint. An inspection of Fig. 6.12 shows that an A_3 is correctly centred at this point.

The contrasts between the city-rich and the city-poor sectors can be examined in terms of Lösch's implication that the number of coincident centres determines the relative size of a particular place[10]. In all instances there are as many or more places that are the centre for a particular number of coincidences in the city-rich sector (Table 6.4).

Table 6.4   Comparison of the city-rich and city-poor sectors (cf. Fig. 6.13) (reprinted from 'The Lösch System of Market Areas: Derivation and Extension.' by K. S. O. Beavon and A. S. Mabin, *Geographical Analysis*, Vol. 7, No. 2 (April 1975), 131–51. Copyright © 1975 by the Ohio State University Press).

No. of coincident centres M	No. of places with M coincident centres		Difference
	City-rich	City-poor	
11	1	0	1
10	0	0	0
9	3	0	3
8	3	1	2
7	4	2	2
6	0	0	0
5	20	8	12
4	10	3	7
3	32	11	21
2	32	32	0
1	57	31	26

A simplified procedure for constructing the Lösch system

It has been shown in this chapter how the Lösch system can be developed *a priori* by recourse to co-ordinate geometry. On the basis of the relationships already shown, a simplified *procedure* for constructing the system of regional market centres (shown in Fig. 6.12) can be presented (Beavon, 1973). As the distance *a* between any two places in the basic lattice can be set to unity, it follows from equation 6.6 that

$$n_r^* = b_r^2 \tag{6.19}$$

For the 30 degree sector $Y'OC$ of the basic lattice (e.g., Fig. 6.11) it is possible to calculate the distance b_r between the origin O and each point in turn. It is therefore possible to calculate n_r^* for each point. The ranked values of n_r^* can be termed Areas A_p ($p = 0, 1, 2, 3, \ldots$). For each point $P(x, y)$ it is then possible to assign an area number A_p that shows that the point $P(x, y)$ is the centre for a particular hexagon H_r. By simple and successive extrapolation it is possible to locate the centres of all other A_p area numbers (for successively $p = 0, 1, 2, 3, \ldots$) in the sector $Y'OC$.

For values of n_r^* between 0 and 150, it has been shown above that there are twenty-two cases[11] where a pair of points $P(x, y)$ and $P'(x', y')$ will yield the same value of n_r^*. In each particular case m the centre of A_m will be located at that alternate point $P(x, y)$ that is already the centre of the greatest number of A_p areas ($p = 0, 1, 2, 3, \ldots, (m - 1)$), or in the case where the number of areas already assigned is equal at the possible alternative locations, the A_m that is being assigned is centred at that alternative that is already a centre of the highest A_p already assigned.

By further extrapolation it is possible to locate the area numbers associated with each point in the sector COX'. The remaining five sectors that complete a full 360 degrees will be identical with the 60 degree sector completed in the manner just described.

In concluding this chapter it may now be of some assistance to readers to clarify and elaborate on the earlier statement by Lösch (1954, p. 117) that his Area Numbers 1, 2 and 3 represent the three smallest hexagons that can be drawn about a service centre (i.e., a point in the basic lattice). Obviously such a statement by itself is erroneous and confusing. This has been partly rectified by drawing attention to the two *implied* constraints that Lösch obviously adhered to (cf. pp. 84–5). It *is* possible to draw an infinite number of hexagons that are for example in-between the sizes of Area Number 1 and Area Number 2. In any event Area Number Zero is smaller than Area Number 1 (Fig. 6.15). However, it would not be

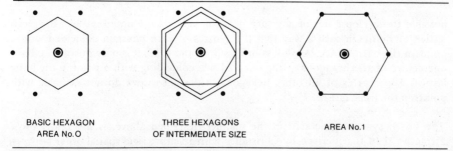

| BASIC HEXAGON | THREE HEXAGONS | AREA No.1 |
| AREA No.0 | OF INTERMEDIATE SIZE | |

Fig. 6.15   Hexagons of a size intermediate to the basic hexagon and the hexagon of Area Number 1 (from Beavon and Mabin, *Tij. Econ. Soc. Geog.* **67**, 1976).

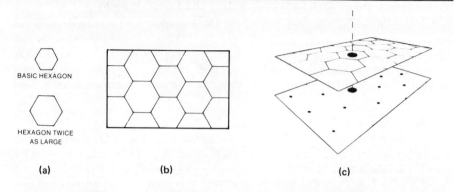

Fig. 6.16   Superimposing a network of hexagons twice as large as the basic hexagon but smaller than Area Number 1 on the basic lattice (after Beavon and Mabin, op. cit., 67, 1976).

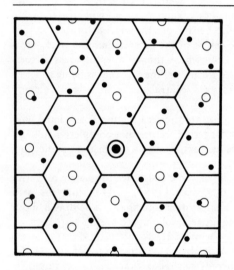

Fig. 6.17   Centres of the superimposed hexagons (open circles) relative to the centres of the basic lattice (black dots) (from Beavon and Mabin, op. cit., 67, 1976).

possible to develop a net of any such hexagon *and* to superimpose it over the *given* lattice of points in such a way that the centres of each hexagon coincided with a point in the basic lattice. As shown in Figs 6.16 and 6.17, it is only possible to have one centre of the hexagons in the selected net coinciding with a point in the basic lattice. The centres of all other hexagons in the net shown do not coincide with points in the basic lattice.

The Lösch system, generated in the manner described above, is inherently more attractive than that derived by Christaller with its more rigid spatial order between higher and lower order centres based on only one type of trade area (K3, K4 or K7) (Dacey, 1965a; Haggett, 1965; Hurst, 1972; Stolper, 1955). However, as stated at the outset of this chapter it appears somewhat inappropriate to equate two places A' and B' say, in Lösch's system merely because they are both places with eight coincident centres of area when the set of areas coincident at A' and B' are different. For example, compare the places $(0, 8)$ and $(0, 6)$ in Fig. 6.12 that are the centres for areas

$$A_0 \quad A_1 \quad A_2 \quad A_5 \quad A_7 \quad A_{18} \quad A_{24} \quad A_{62}$$

and

$$A_0 \quad A_1 \quad A_2 \quad A_4 \quad A_5 \quad A_{11} \quad A_{14} \quad A_{37}$$

respectively. The equality of eight coincident centres alone should not be sufficient reason for equating these two places as in a hierarchy (as suggested by Yeates and Garner, 1971; and implicitly by Haggett, 1965). The different sets of commodities reflected by the different centres of area reflecting associated and varying threshold areas indicate the A' and B' are different types of place.

In contemplating the application of the Lösch system on an intra-urban scale, it would appear more accurate to describe the city-rich and city-poor sectors of the Löschian scheme as sectors rich and poor in the number of services offered. The concept of service-rich and service-poor sectors or business-rich and business-poor sectors also appears apposite if the arrangement of shopping centres within a large city or metropolitan area is to be considered. It has been suggested by Dacey (1965b) that the Lösch system not only holds a wide variety of locational and functional relations for central place activities but provides a broader and more penetrating basis for the study of urban systems as opposed to the inflexible stepped hierarchical model. Furthermore it has recently been suggested by Parr (1973, p. 208) that the interpretation of Lösch on an intra-metropolitan scale may be particularly appropriate as factors which lead to inconsistencies and possible distortions at the regional level will tend to be absent or diminished at the intra-metropolitan scale. The development of an intra-metropolitan model of the location of tertiary activities based essentially on the Lösch model, the geometry of which has now been derived, is presented in the chapter that follows.

Notes

1. The error follows equation 8C of the Mills–Lav (1964) paper. It is related to the statement that $a - bk > 0$, that in turn gives rise to an assumption. This leads to the incorrect specification of demands at the frontier of the market area of a firm (Hartwick, 1973).
2. The statement that the size of any market area is equal to $a^2 n \sqrt{(3 \div 2)}$ (Lösch, 1954, pp. 116 and 118) is incorrect as published.
3. It is possible for more than two sets of values for l_h and k_h to yield the same value of n_h^*, e.g., A_{184} has $n_h^* = 637$ with values of (l_h, k_h) equal to $(9\frac{1}{2}, 13\frac{1}{2})$, $(7, 14)$ or $(2\frac{1}{2}, 14\frac{1}{2})$ when $h = 204$, 216, and 226 with values of $m = 14$, 15, and 15 respectively.
4. The line OY' and OX' are identical. If the two sectors are each to be equal 30 degree sectors then all centres on the line OY' and all centres to the left of but not on the line OC (Fig. 6.11) should be part of the city-rich sector. Similarly, the city-poor sector would contain all centres on the line OC and all centres to the left of but not on the line OX'. This, however, would conflict with the *procedure* Lösch adopted in locating the centres of Areas A_0 to A_{150}.
5. In practice if the centres are being plotted by hand no difficulty in coping with the 'rotation' should be encountered. A procedure for finding the third centre and thereafter

all centres for a particular area number has been incorporated in a Fortran program written by the author. The program LOSCH generates the Area Number numbers associated with each point in a 60 degree city-rich and city-poor sector of the lattice up to and including A_{339}.

6. Note that the centre of A_{25} is located at (2½, 4½) and the 25 shown alongside the point (3, 5) in Lösch's diagram (Fig. 6.9) should be read as a 2 and a 5 as now shown in Fig. 6.12.

7. In the event (not encountered up to and including A_{150}) of two places being the centres of the same number of coincident areas *and* where the highest area numbers are the same the choice would be similarly based on a consideration of the next pair of values. The case of A_{55} is a special case and Lösch's decision to locate it at (6½, 6½) in preference to (½, 7½) appears to be arbitrary.

8. A_0 is common to all points and is not included in the summation.

9. Both A_{156} and A_{161} have alternative pairs of co-ordinates. The constraint imposed by the requirement that coincidence be maximised excludes (5, 13) and (2½, 13½) as the respective alternates.

10. The relative sizes of places in Lösch's system of market areas might be extrapolated on the basis of varying assumptions regarding the relationship between n_p^*, A_p and possible population figures (e.g., Beckmann, 1958; Henderson, 1972; Parr, 1973). This book is not concerned with such considerations.

11. Readers who are not yet clear on what is meant by the term 'alternative centres' or who do not understand how they arise are referred to Beavon and Mabin, 1976.

Chapter 7

Towards an alternative theory of tertiary activity

Certain aspects of the theoretical work of Christaller, Berry and Garrison, and Lösch are more appealing than other parts. The *emergence* of central places of lower order in the Christallerian landscape is appealing as opposed to the *assumption* of a complete set of central place locations as an early step in the Lösch model. However, the Lösch model, developed as it is from the lowest order central place *upwards*, is more appealing in a dynamic and real world sense than the models of Christaller and Berry and Garrison. The latter models are developed *downwards* from high order centres, presupposing the development of the population surface as a *fait accompli* before the first central place appears. Implicit in the Lösch model is the necessity to assume an *unbounded* isotropic plane, whereas in both the Christaller and Berry and Garrison models some concept of *bounded* or limited space is permitted — because both excess and normal profit situations are catered for in the downward development of their models. It appears both desirable, and possible, to incorporate the attractive features of the three models in the modified Lösch model to be presented here.

In setting out to develop an alternative model of the location of tertiary activities the major objective is to achieve a closer resemblance to the observed continuum of shopping centres than is achieved by the stepped hierarchy models. Before proceeding it is both desirable and necessary to take cognisance of certain pertinent criticisms that have been levelled at the Lösch model by Curry (1962); of certain empirical findings of Berry and Garrison (1958b) relating to excess profit situations; and also to incorporate some heuristic aspects of observed shopping centre compositions, in particular the distinction between 'shopping' retailers and convenience commodity retailers.

Four major criticisms have been levelled at the original Lösch model by Curry (1962). Briefly they refer to:

1. The use of an unbounded plane surface;
2. The unreasoned assumption that all activities occur in the central metropolis;
3. The lack of consideration given to multiproduct firms;
4. The assumption that the delivered price of central commodities increases with delivery distance.

Observation of urban systems in Snohomish County has led to the conclusion that as the number of businesses increase the possibility of earning excess profits per establishment diminishes (Fig. 7.1). Two conclusions have been drawn:

1. That excess profits are relatively less significant in larger urban centres than in small centres;

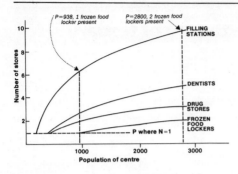

Fig. 7.1 Rates of duplication of activities in Snohomish County (after Berry and Garrison, *Econ. Geog.*, 34, 1958b).

2. Over time the urban system demonstrates a trend towards some optimal condition in which excess profits are non-existent (Berry and Garrison, 1958b, p. 309).

The trends reflected by these conclusions are supported on theoretical grounds by Isard (1956) and tacitly by Allpass *et al.* (1967). As such, in developing an alternative model the retention of Berry and Garrison's threshold concept appears to have certain merit.

It is generally recognised that there are two major groups of retail commodities termed convenience and 'shopping' commodities. These groups have already been incorporated in discussions of the implicit aspects of the theory of tertiary activity (Garner, 1966, pp. 14–16). Furthermore it has long been accepted (Nelson, 1958) that these two groups of commodities are sold by retail firms that operate in different ways. The different methods of operation are reflected not only in the scale of operation, but also in the respective choices of location for business premises. Generally shops dealing essentially in convenience commodities tend to be small and choose locations near pedestrian generators of which 'shopping' commodity stores are good examples (Nelson, 1958, pp. 48–9). It can be argued that small speciality shops will be located in much the same way as convenience shops and will select locations where it will be possible to nest within the customer attraction of larger more generative businesses.

It will be recalled (from Chapter 2) that in 1958 the work of Lösch was rejected by Berry and Garrison (1958c) because of the belief that Lösch excluded the possibility of a firm earning excess profits. In setting out to develop a model of the location of intra-metropolitan tertiary activity based on the Lösch model, it is imperative that the notion of no excess profits in the Lösch system be dispelled. Lösch himself never excluded the possibility. On the contrary he commented (Lösch, 1954, p. 120):

The most important result of the preceding argument is that with discontinuous settlement the possible size of the market areas and the number of settlements they contain also grows discontinuously. This, again, makes surplus profits possible. For if sales in 32 settlements, say, were required to make a certain commodity profitable, area no. 13 with 31 settlements would be too small. But the next area is the unnecessarily large market area 14, with 36 settlements, so that sales must extend to 36 settlements. The demand curve would then intersect the cost curve instead of merely touching it, and surplus profits would thus arise in this industry. Such moderate surplus profits are actually the rule for it would be pure chance if the demand curve in its jumps should still 'just touch the cost curve'.

As Lösch specifically allows for excess profits[1] it is in order to re-examine his work with a view to extending it into the field of tertiary activity.

Using essentially the same approach as originally used by Lösch, it is possible to consider how shopping centres containing varying types of business will emerge in an intra-metropolitan system. In the first instance the model will be developed under a set of constraints that imply *inter alia* perfect knowledge by the entrepreneurs. However, once the model has been developed it will be possible to heed the plea that models should take cognisance of the fact that most entrepreneurs and consumers operate under conditions of imperfect knowledge (Johnston, 1968b).

The assumptions on which the constrained intra-urban model will initially be developed are:

1. That an urban settlement with its own economic base sufficient to maintain the growth of its population is located at some point on an isotropic plane;
2. That as the population grows it will spread outwards equally in all directions from the central point of the urban place with density ρ (this follows from the first assumption of isotropism);
3. That the first business of the smallest business type A_0 with threshold $_A n_0 = 1$ and the first business of each of a set of possible business types A_i, with threshold requirements $_A n_i$ ($i = 1, 2, 3, \ldots$) will always locate at the centre of the urban place;
4. That all businesses in the set A_i of business types will be able to make at least normal profits in the long run;
5. That the second business of type A_0 will select a location before the second business of any other business type A_i ($i = 1, 2, 3, \ldots$) selects a location;
6. That where a choice of alternative locations for the second firm of business type A_i ($i = 1, 2, 3, \ldots$) exists, the choice will be made as follows: first, the firm will locate at the alternative location that is in the business-rich sector; secondly when the alternatives are both in the business-rich sector, the firm will locate at that site that is already the site of the largest number of different business types (to benefit from the economies of agglomeration);
7. That possible initial losses can be written off if over a long period of time sufficient excess profits are made to at least balance such initial losses;
8. That the costs of procuring supplies from wholesalers are averaged across all firms dealing in the same commodities and all other costs are assumed equal;
9. That ease of movement in all directions is equal and proportional to distance;
10. That a business type A_i is distinguished from a business type A_j ($i \neq j$) by its threshold requirements as a business, although both businesses may *appear* to deal in the same general type of commodity or service;
11. That a set of business types B_j can exist with threshold $_B n_j$ ($j = 1, 2, 3, \ldots$) but $_B n_j \neq {_A n_i}$ for any values of $i = 0, 1, 2, 3, \ldots$ and $j = 1, 2, 3, 4, \ldots$;
12. That the first firm of business type B_j will always locate at the centre of the urban place;
13. That B_j firms will only locate where excess profit will be possible over long periods of time;
14. That the threshold values of $_A n_i$ ($i = 0, 1, 2, 3, \ldots$) and $_B n_j$ ($j = 1, 2, 3, \ldots$) must be integers (although they may represent specified units of population).

The concept of threshold

The term threshold in urban geography is normally associated with the development of the theory of tertiary activity in which it is clearly stated that there must be some minimum size of market below which a place will be unable to supply a central commodity. Where sales are just sufficient to support the supply of a central commodity from a central place, the threshold requirements of the firm are met and normal profits will be earned. The threshold can be expressed as the lower limit of the *range* of a central commodity that encloses the minimum amount of necessary purchasing power for a firm to enter the market. The *range* represents the distance beyond which a firm is unable to attract custom and/or beyond which it is uneconomic to deliver its commodities or provide its services.

When considering the complete and even distribution of population on an isotropic plane, population, purchasing power and threshold area are all directly proportionate to each other. Obviously, in the real world this is not always the case. On the one hand in the real world small areas of a city, with relatively low population densities, where wealthy families reside can provide large amounts of purchasing power. On the other hand large areas of the same city inhabited by poor families living in high density developments normally provide relatively small amounts of purchasing power.

The concept of isotropism as employed in central place theory also implies that persons will all purchase the same amounts of a central commodity. In the real world this is not so and it is acceptable to state the threshold requirement of a particular commodity in terms of population or purchasing power. However, if the threshold requirements so expressed for each of the N commodities offered by tertiary firms in a real city were summed, the total population or purchasing power so obtained would normally exceed the total population or purchasing power of the city. The reason for this is simple: a high order central commodity needs to be central to a large population not because everyone will buy it, but because somewhere in such a large population there will be sufficient numbers of persons who will find the firm accessible and who will provide the required *threshold sales* to allow the firm to earn normal profits. In the real world situation purchasing power, threshold area and threshold sales are not likely to be directly proportionate.

Generally, the lower the threshold requirement in terms of population and purchasing power the lower is the order of a commodity and the higher the probability that a person (or a family unit) will make a purchase. The probability that an individual (or a family unit) will purchase a commodity in a particular time period tends to decrease as the necessity for or general utility of the commodity decreases. The frequency of making a purchase decreases as order of the commodity increases. Whereas the cost of a commodity can be related with the order of the commodity, cost itself is not a good index of either order, or probability, i.e., utility of a purchase. Nor is it a good index of threshold. Effective demand, however, will give the extent of the threshold area (B. Goodall, 1972, p. 32). For example, where a commodity is demanded by only four persons in every thousand in a time period y, the probability of an individual making a purchase is 0.004. If the threshold requirements of a firm dealing in such a commodity is 1,000 sales, in the same time period y, then its threshold area would have to be such that it encloses 250,000 persons.

Whereas the term threshold is normally employed when discussing a particular commodity it can also be used to define the requirements for a particular type of business. Experience has shown that for a particular commodity, suppose a summer frock, some people will shop only at department stores, others at popular clothing-chain stores and others at small speciality dress shops. In considering the intra-urban business system the concern is with different types of businesses that need not necessarily be acceptable alternatives to all shoppers (the same viewpoint has been taken by Parr and Denike, 1970). In the ensuing discussion both the concepts of varying probabilities of purchasing and the varying nature of different types of business will be taken into account.

The relationships between the terms so far discussed can be expressed more succinctly as a series of equations. Let the probability p of a purchase from a particular type of business A_i be p_i ($1 \geqslant p_i \geqslant 0$). The threshold population $_An_i$ can then be calculated from

$$_An_i = {_st_i}/p_i \qquad (7.1)$$

where $_st_i$ is the threshold sales necessary for business type A_i. If the population density ρ is known then the threshold area $_at_i$ for business type i can be calculated from

$$_at_i = {_An_i}/\rho \qquad (7.2)$$

and if the threshold area is known

$$_An_i = {_at_i}\rho \qquad (7.3)$$

The case of the business type A_0 with the smallest possible threshold population $_An_0$ can now be considered in detail.

Location and profits

Consider assumption one (above) as implemented. As the population P increases over time T it will reach a size P_T relative to the threshold population requirements $_An_0$ of the smallest business type A_0, such that

$$P_T < {_An_0} \qquad (7.4)$$

and any firm establishing itself then would have to be satisfied with subnormal profits (Fig. 7.2a).

Alternatively the population P may reach a size P_T such that

$$P_T = {_An_0} \qquad (7.5)$$

and normal profits can be earned (Fig. 7.2b), or if

$$P_T > {_An_0} \qquad (7.6)$$

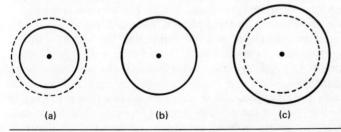

(a)   (b)   (c)

Fig. 7.2   The relationship between the threshold area of A_0 (dashed line) and the expanding area of the urban place (solid line) (from Beavon, S. *Afr. Geog. J.*, 56, 1974a).

excess profits can be earned (Fig. 7.2c). Which of the three conditions will prevail depends *inter alia* on the acumen of the entrepreneur and his knowledge of the threshold requirements. If an entrepreneur wishes to pre-empt the market he may decide to operate on sub-normal profits for a period of time. Usually such a decision is based on knowledge, or hope, that the rate of growth of the population and delayed establishment of competition will yield a period of time during which excess profits will be made to at least balance the initial losses. The threshold requirements of A_0 can be defined as a unit of population.

Just as the first entrepreneur may forego normal profits in order to pre-empt the best location, so too might his future competitors (in accordance with assumption 4 the competitors can only compete for the excess profits that the existing firm is making). Only when the population has increased to 7 units of population will it be possible for the first business of business type A_0, i.e., $A_{0,1}$, to be completely surrounded by similar businesses $A_{0,j}$ ($j = 2, 3, \ldots 7$) such that all $A_{0,j}$ ($j = 1, 2, \ldots 7$) will be able to make normal profits. It follows from assumption 4 that in the long run all businesses of business type A_0 except those on or near the periphery of the urban place will be located at the centre of a hexagonal trade area. The threshold area $_a t_0$ of A_0 is therefore given by

$$_a t_0 = \frac{a^2\sqrt{3}}{2} \tag{7.7}$$

(from equation 6.5)

and the threshold population $_A n_0$ by

$$_A n_0 = \frac{\rho a^2\sqrt{3}}{2} \tag{7.8}$$

(from equation 7.3)

where ρ is the population density and is constant throughout the urban area. In practice where ρ is known it would be possible to calculate the distance a that would satisfy assumption 4 from

$$a^2 = \frac{2_A n_0}{\rho\sqrt{3}} \tag{7.9}$$

For convenience a can be set to unity and as ρ is a constant it need not be considered explicitly in the discussion that follows.

Suppose that only one other business of type A_0, say $A_{0,2}$, pre-empts a location at a stage when the population of the urban place has exceeded $_A n_0$ and the urban place has a radius a. Such an entrepreneur might choose any location at distance a from $A_{0,1}$ (Fig.7.3a) in accordance with assumption 4. The trade area of $A_{0,1}$ is now divided by a straight line at right angles to a line connecting $A_{0,1}$ and $A_{0,2}$. In this situation $A_{0,1}$ continues to make excess profits. If instead of only $A_{0,2}$ pre-empting a location two businesses $A_{0,2}$ and $A_{0,3}$ pre-empt locations at the same time then a situation as represented in Fig. 7.3b might occur. Similarly, if the maximum of six entrepreneurs eventually pre-empt locations or do so at the same time the situation would be as shown in Fig. 7.3c. If the six entrepreneurs pre-empt their locations at different times then, given continuing urban growth, a sequence such as shown in Fig. 7.4 might occur. It is possible for the firm $A_{0,1}$ to earn excess profits even after four other firms ($A_{0,2}$ to $A_{0,5}$) have established themselves and are also earning

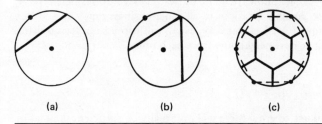

Fig. 7.3 The emergence of additional firms of A_0 with size of urban place held constant. The dashed hexagon represents the threshold area for the next type of business A_1 (from Beavon, op. cit., 56, 1974a).

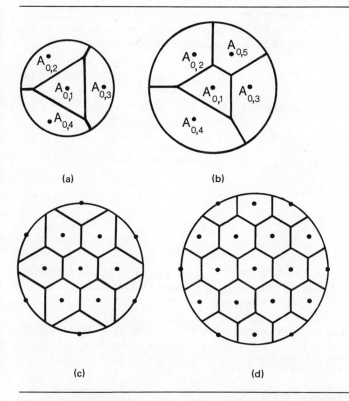

Fig. 7.4 The relationship between different firms of A_0 establishing themselves at different times as the urban area continues to grow (from Beavon, op. cit., 56, 1974a).

excess profits (Fig. 7.4b). Even after the urban area has increased its radius to $a\sqrt{3}$ it is possible for as many as six A_0 firms to continue making excess profits (Fig. 7.4c). It is only once the urban area has grown to a radius of $a\sqrt{4}$, and all business sites have been occupied by A_0 firms, that temporarily no excess profits will be made by A_0 firms (Fig. 7.4d).

From the above discussion, and from what is implicit in assumption 5 and assumption 4 (in that order), it follows that the outward spread of business type A_0 effectively determines the possible locations of all other business types A_i. Furthermore, the possible locations for all business types A_0 will form a 60 degree lattice with distance a separating nearest neighbours from each other.

The location of business types A_i $(i > 0)$

As the urban place continues to grow there will eventually be sufficient population to support a business type A_1 at the centre (i.e., $A_{1,1}$). An initial competitor, $A_{1,2}$, must locate in accordance with the general assumptions given above. The location that can be selected must allow for a trade area that will be greater than that required for the smaller business type A_0, but small enough to allow normal profits to be achieved as soon as possible. Such a location will be the one that is second nearest to the central location. Given the finite set of possible locations, determined by the emerging lattice of A_0 centres, this distance must necessarily be $a\sqrt{3}$. The threshold area $_a t_1$ of A_1 is obtained from equation 6.4 that becomes

$$_a t_1 = \frac{(a\sqrt{3})^2\sqrt{3}}{2} \tag{7.10}$$

The threshold population n_1 is given by

$$_A n_1 = \frac{\rho(a\sqrt{3})^2\sqrt{3}}{2} \tag{7.11}$$

(from equation 7.3)

The ratio $_A n_1 / _A n_0$ is given by

$$_A n_1 / _A n_0 = [2^{-1}3(\rho a^2\sqrt{3})][2(\rho a^2\sqrt{3})^{-1}]$$

(from equations 7.11 and 7.7)

$$= 3 \quad \text{(cf. Table 6.3)} \tag{7.12}$$

The threshold of business type A_1 is therefore three times as great as that required by business type A_0. As all $A_{1,j}$ firms $(j = 1, 2, 3, \ldots)$ are required to make normal profits in the long run they must locate at places that are $a\sqrt{3}$ distant from each other.

Similarly, business type A_2 will eventually be able to make normal profits at the centre of the urban place and its competitors will locate at a distance of $2a$ (or $a\sqrt{4}$) apart. The threshold area $_a t_2$ and threshold population $_A n_2$ relative to $_a t_0$ and $_A n_0$ is given by the ratio

$$_A n_2 / _A n_0 = [2^{-1}4(\rho a^2\sqrt{3})][2(\rho a^2\sqrt{3})^{-1}]$$

$$= 4 \quad \text{(cf., Table 6.3)} \tag{7.13}$$

The distance $2a$ is equal to the distance between any place in the lattice and its third nearest neighbour. A general statement of the relative location of the second firm of any A_i business relative to the first firm can now be made, viz., the possible locations of the second firm of business type A_i will be at those places separated from each other by a distance equal to that between the central location and its $(i + 1)$th nearest neighbour. When this procedure yields two or more places that are equidistant from the centre but not from each other, the choice of location is made

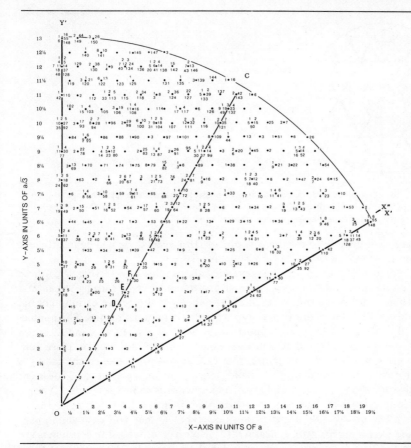

Fig. 7.5   The location of shopping centres. The numbers indicate that a place is the centre of the threshold area for particular business types A_i with i in the range 1 to 150. All places are centres for A_0 and the origin O is the location of each A_i (i = 0, 1, 2, 3, . . ., 150) (from Beavon, op. cit., 56, 1974a).

by implementing assumption 6. The net result will be the production of the business-rich and business-poor sectors equivalent to the city-rich and city-poor sectors of the Lösch model. If *area numbers* are read as *business types* then Fig. 6.12 (reproduced here as Fig. 7.5) can be interpreted as the distribution of 151 A-type businesses in an urban area that has a radius of $a\sqrt{511}$.

The emergence of successive firms

As the urban place grows, so it will become possible to support different types of business A_i at its centre even before it is possible for more than one firm of A_0 to earn even normal profits. Consider the stage in growth when the radius of the built-up area is successively a, and $a\sqrt{4}$ (Figs 7.3c and 7.6). Furthermore, assume that all possible sites of A_0 can only be, *and are*, pre-empted if the sites are within or on the boundary of the urban place. When the radius of the urban place is $a\sqrt{1}$ (Fig. 7.3c) it will be large enough to support one firm of A_0 at normal profits. Six other A_0 firms will earn subnormal profits. A single firm of A_1, located at the centre of the

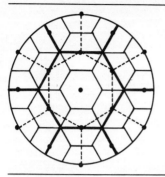

Fig. 7.6 The urban place with radius $2a$ when all possible business sites at this stage of growth have been pre-empted. The threshold areas of A_0, A_1, and A_2 are shown by fine, dashed, and bold lines respectively (from Beavon, op. cit., 56, 1974a).

urban place, will be able to earn excess profits. However, there will be insufficient population to support a firm of A_2 at normal profits.

By the time the built-up area has extended to a radius of $a\sqrt{4}$ (Fig. 7.6) there will be seven firms of A_0 earning normal profits and twelve earning subnormal profits. There will be one firm of each of A_1 and A_2 at the centre earning normal profits and six firms of each of these types earning subnormal profits. The population will also be large enough to support single firms of A_3, A_4, A_5, and A_6 at the centre of the urban place and all will earn excess profits. As the urban place continues to grow so firms at the centre, that earn excess profits when the radius is $a\sqrt{4}$, will earn only normal profits as additional firms of the same type locate at pre-emptive locations on the periphery. The sequence is shown in Table 7.1 for a set of discrete cases as the radius of the urban place increases from $a\sqrt{1}$ to $a\sqrt{13}$.

The number of *different* firms of business type A_i that will earn subnormal, normal, and excess profits can be measured[2]. However, as far as the consumers are concerned the firm is operative and caters for their demands. The *number* of firms of each type can easily be measured making use of Fig. 7.5 that shows the location of all A_i firms from A_0 to A_{150} for a 60 degree sector of the urban place[3].

For convenience, as only a portion of Fig. 7.5 need be considered, that portion is shown as Fig. 7.7. For any radius the number of business types that exist outside the centre of the urban place will be six times as many as those found in the 60 degree business-rich—business-poor sector that is shown above (note that those places on the line OX' are excluded as it represents the start of the next business-rich sector). For each business type located outside the centre there will be one firm at the centre. In addition it will be possible for a number of business types to locate at the centre and earn at least normal profits. If it is assumed that firms *will* be established at the centre *if and only if* normal profits are available, then the types of these additional firms can be calculated by comparing the area of the urban place at any stage with the threshold area for each A_i firm. A simple example should make this clear.

The area of the urban place U at any time T is given by

$$U_T = \pi r^2 \tag{7.14}$$

If the radius r of the urban place is given as $a\sqrt{36}$, then assuming a set to unity

$$U_T = 113.1 \tag{7.15}$$

Table 7.1 The number of firms of business type A_i that will earn subnormal (S), normal (N), or excess profits (E) on the assumption that all pre-emptive locations at radius r have been taken up, and that firms will establish themselves if normal profits can be made (after Beavon, op. cit., 56, 1974a).

	A_0			A_1			A_2			A_3			A_4			A_5			A_6			A_7	A_8	A_9	A_{10}	A_{11}	A_{12}	A_{13}	A_{14}	A_{15}	A_{16}	A_{17}	A_{18}
r	S	N	E	S	N	E	S	N	E	S	N	E	S	N	E	S	N	E	S	N	E	E	E	E	E	E	E	E	E	E	E	E	E
$a\sqrt{1}$	6	1			1																												
$a\sqrt{3}$	6	1	6		1	6		1			1																						
$a\sqrt{4}$	12	7		6	1		6	1			1			1			1																
$a\sqrt{7}$	12	13	6		1	6	6	1		6	1			1			1			1		1	1	1									
$a\sqrt{9}$	18	19		6	1	6		1	6	6	1		6	1			1			1		1	1	1	1								
$a\sqrt{12}$	6	19	18	12	7		6	1	6		1	6	6	1		6	1			1		1	1	1	1	1	1	1	1	1	1	1	
$a\sqrt{13}$	18	31	6	12	7		6	1	6		1	6	6	1		6	1		6	1		1	1	1	1	1	1	1	1	1	1	1	

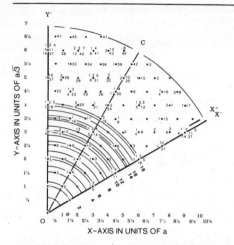

Fig. 7.7 The successive sizes of the urban area, represented here by a 60 degree sector, that will enclose at least one more business site (i.e., at least six more for the whole urban area). The boundary numbers (figures set parallel with OX') correspond with the increment numbers (*Inc*) shown in Table 7.2. The outer boundary of sector $Y'OX'$ is drawn with radius $a\sqrt{140.86}$ (from Beavon, op. cit., 56, 1974a).

As ρ is a constant the threshold population for any business type A_i is proportional to the area of its corresponding hexagonal trade area. The threshold area $_at_i$ can therefore be calculated from equation 6.4. The distance between any two A_i firms (for a specific value i) is b^2 and is obtained from Table 6.3. In this way the threshold area of A_{45} is given by:

$$_at_{45} = \frac{129\sqrt{3}}{2}$$

$$= 111.7 \tag{7.16}$$

Business type 45 located at the centre could earn normal profits as its threshold area, equation 7.16, is less than the area of the urban place, equation 7.15. Similarly the threshold area for A_{46} can be calculated

$$_at_{46} = \frac{133\sqrt{3}}{2}$$

$$= 115.2 \tag{7.17}$$

As the threshold area required by A_{46} exceeds the area of the urban place (equation 7.15) such a firm will not be established at the centre of the urban place (i.e., in terms of the assumption made at the outset of this procedure for calculating the number of different firms in the urban place). It can be concluded that there will be one firm of each A_i ($i = 0, 1, 2, \ldots, 45$) business type established at the centre. This procedure can be used to establish how many business types exist at each successive increment of growth in the urban area. Again, for convenience, an increment in radius can be confined to that which is just sufficient to include at least six more places on the periphery of the urban area (one more place if only the sector $Y'OX''$ is being considered). The results of applying this procedure for nineteen successive increments in radius from an initial radius of $a\sqrt{1}$, and a special case when the radius is $a\sqrt{140.86}$, are shown in Table 7.2.

Examination of Table 7.2 shows that with each increment I there will be an addition of six firms of business type A_I. The increment in the number of other business types A_i $(i = 0, 1, 2, \ldots (I-1))$ is not regular, neither is the increment in the number of additional firms A_i $(i > I)$ that establish themselves at the centre for the first time (on the assumption that they will do so if normal profits can be made). Essentially the number of business types that can be supported at the centre of the urban place increases more rapidly than the number of business types that can be supported beyond the centre. The implication is that under the set of assumptions the effective spread of business types from the centre to other locations is slowed down as the urban place grows. Whereas the single business type A_{10}, with the largest threshold requirement when the radius is $a\sqrt{7}$, is increased to seven firms after seven increments, the firm A_{31} that has the highest threshold requirements when the radius is $a\sqrt{25}$ is only increased to seven firms after twenty-one increments (i.e., *Inc.* is thirty-one, Table 7.2). If the rate of growth of the urban place decreases then effectively the time period, between a business opening at the centre and the opening of a second firm of the same type on the periphery of the built-up area, is increased still further.

The location of business types B_j

As the set of business types A_i are constrained in their choice of location their threshold values $_An_i$ $(i = 0, 1, 2, 3, \ldots)$ are necessarily discrete and discontinuous. It is possible for firms of business type B_j (as defined in assumption 11) to choose a location, both at and beyond the centre of the urban place, in such a way that they are assured of excess profits over long periods of time (and so satisfy assumption 13). Provided each firm of business type B_j chooses to establish itself at a location already occupied by a firm of business type A_i, where

$$A^{n_i} > {}_B n_j > A^{n_{(i-1)}} \tag{7.18}$$

then the firm B_j will be assured of excess profits over long periods of time.

The situation described is possible because the B_j firm (say $B_{j,1}$) that locates in the manner described will experience no spatial competition. The radius of the B_j trade area will be less than the distance between the associated A_i firm and its point of indifference $(b_i/2)$ with its nearest A_i neighbour at which another B_j firm $(B_{j,2})$ may locate, where

$$_B n_{j,1} = {}_B n_{j,2} < {}_A n_i \tag{7.19}$$

It is also possible for a firm B_k $(k > j$ or $j > k)$ to locate at the same place provided that the relationship between the B-type firms and the A_i firms already located at the place satisfy inequality 7.18 and either 7.20 or 7.21 below

$$_B n_j < {}_B n_k < {}_A n_i \tag{7.20}$$

$$_B n_k < {}_B n_j < {}_A n_i \tag{7.21}$$

Notwithstanding the nomenclature of A_i and B_j types of business that has been adopted for convenience of argument, no categorical differences in either the type or the quality of commodities dealt in is implied. The introduction of a set of B_j business types does not mean that a location that has an A_k firm will now also be a

Table 7.2   The number of A_i firms within the urban area at different stages of growth. Successi increments of urban growth (*Inc*) are such that the radius of the urban area (r) will increa sufficiently to enclose at least six additional sites† for A_0 firms‡ (after Beavon, op. cit., **56**, 1974a).

Inc.	r	Values of i																											
		0	1	2	3	4	5	6	7	8	9	10	11	12	13	14	15	16	17	18	19	20	21	22	23	24	25	26	27	28
0	$a\sqrt{1}$	7	1																											
1	$a\sqrt{3}$	13	7	1	1	1																								
2	$a\sqrt{4}$	19	7	7	1	1	1	1																						
3	$a\sqrt{7}$	31	7	7	7	1	1	1	1	1	1																			
4	$a\sqrt{9}$	37	13	7	7	7	1	1	1	1	1	1	1	1	1															
5	$a\sqrt{12}$	43	19	13	7	7	7	1	1	1	1	1	1	1	1	1	1	1	1											
6	$a\sqrt{13}$	55	19	13	7	7	7	7	1	1	1	1	1	1	1	1	1	1	1											
7	$a\sqrt{16}$	61	19	19	7	7	7	7	1	1	1	1	1	1	1	1	1	1	1	1	1	1	1							
8	$a\sqrt{19}$	73	19	19	7	7	7	7	7	7	1	1	1	1	1	1	1	1	1	1	1	1	1	1	1	1				
9	$a\sqrt{21}$	85	31	19	13	7	7	7	7	7	7	1	1	1	1	1	1	1	1	1	1	1	1	1	1	1	1	1	1	1
10	$a\sqrt{25}$	91	31	19	13	7	7	7	7	7	7	7	1	1	1	1	1	1	1	1	1	1	1	1	1	1	1	1	1	1
11	$a\sqrt{27}$	97	37	19	13	13	7	7	7	7	7	7	7	1	1	1	1	1	1	1	1	1	1	1	1	1	1	1	1	1
12	$a\sqrt{28}$	109	37	31	19	13	7	7	7	7	7	7	7	7	1	1	1	1	1	1	1	1	1	1	1	1	1	1	1	1
13	$a\sqrt{31}$	121	37	31	19	13	7	7	7	7	7	7	7	7	7	1	1	1	1	1	1	1	1	1	1	1	1	1	1	1
14	$a\sqrt{36}$	127	43	37	19	19	13	7	7	7	7	7	7	7	7	7	1	1	1	1	1	1	1	1	1	1	1	1	1	1
15	$a\sqrt{37}$	139	43	37	19	19	13	7	7	7	7	7	7	7	7	7	1	1	1	1	1	1	1	1	1	1	1	1	1	1
16	$a\sqrt{39}$	151	55	37	19	19	13	13	7	7	7	7	7	7	7	7	7	1	1	1	1	1	1	1	1	1	1	1	1	1
17	$a\sqrt{43}$	163	55	37	19	19	13	13	7	7	7	7	7	7	7	7	7	7	1	1	1	1	1	1	1	1	1	1	1	1
18	$a\sqrt{48}$	169	61	43	19	19	19	13	13	7	7	7	7	7	7	7	7	7	7	1	1	1	1	1	1	1	1	1	1	1
19	$a\sqrt{49}$	187	61	55	19	19	19	13	13	7	7	7	7	7	7	7	7	7	7	1	1	1	1	1	1	1	1	1	1	1
	$a\sqrt{140.86}$	511	163	133	61	55	37	37	31	31	19	19	19	19	19	13	13	13	13	7	7	7	7	7	7	7	7	7	7	

† The value of $r = \sqrt{140.86}$ is a special case and is discussed in the text.
‡ Any site *on* the boundary of the urban area is assumed to be enclosed.

suitable or possible location for all other A_i firms ($i = 0, 1, 2, \ldots (k-1)$). The constraints set out in inequalities 7.18 to 7.21 prevent this. Consider the following three examples at the locations D, E, and F in Fig. 7.5. Place D is a centre for A_0, A_3, and A_{19} with $_An_i$ values of 1, 7, and 49 respectively. Although any B_j firm may consider establishing itself at D the strictures of assumption 13 as formalised in inequality 7.18 will prevent this. The firm A_{19} with $_An_{19}$ of 49 has the highest threshold requirements of those firms that are located at D. A firm B_j with $_Bn_j$ of 48 does not qualify to establish itself at D as such a firm does not satisfy the constraints of inequality 7.18 because $_An_{18}$ is 48. However, a B_j firm with $_Bn_j$ values of 6 or 5 could effectively *nest* in the trade area of the A_3 firm because

$$_An_3 = 7 > (6 \text{ or } 5) > {}_An_2 = 4 \tag{7.22}$$

Similarly, B_j firms with $_Bn_j$ values of 15, 14, and 8 could establish themselves at place E, and B_j firms with $_Bn_j$ values of 80, 26, and 8 could establish themselves at place F.

It is envisaged that the A_i business types would include multi-product firms such as supermarkets, department and variety stores. The multi-product concept can also be extended to include free-standing shopping malls under limited management. The B_j businesses are envisaged as essentially single-product speciality firms. However, it would not be desirable to categorise A_i and B_j firms solely on this basis. Argument has been cited that single-product firms that reach a competitive state of equilibrium accord with acceptable theories of the retail firm (Berry and Garrison, 1958c). On this basis the behaviour of the B_j businesses earning excess profits even over long periods of time can be accepted. The multi-product firm appears to behave in a more sophisticated manner (Holton, 1957). Such a firm achieves an equilibrium only after the sum of marginal costs of all products is equal to the marginal revenues derived from the sale of each product, i.e., when marginal profit

Values of i																															
30	31	32	33	34	35	36	37	38	39	40	41	42	43	44	45	46	47	48	49	50	51	52	53	54	55	56	57	58	59	60	61→150
1	1																														
1	1	1	1	1																											
1	1	1	1	1	1																										
1	1	1	1	1	1	1	1	1	1																						
1	1	1	1	1	1	1	1	1	1	1	1	1	1	1	1																
1	1	1	1	1	1	1	1	1	1	1	1	1	1	1	1																
1	1	1	1	1	1	1	1	1	1	1	1	1	1	1	1	1	1														
1	1	1	1	1	1	1	1	1	1	1	1	1	1	1	1	1	1	1	1	1											
1	1	1	1	1	1	1	1	1	1	1	1	1	1	1	1	1	1	1	1	1	1	1	1	1	1	1					
1	1	1	1	1	1	1	1	1	1	1	1	1	1	1	1	1	1	1	1	1	1	1	1	1	1	1	1	1	1	1	
7	7	7	7	7	7	7	7	7	7	7	7	7	7	7	7	7	7	7	1	1	1	1	1	1	1	1	1	1	1	1	1→1

is zero under the conditions of perfect competition. The A_i business types all have a period during which excess profits can be earned and achieve normal profits only in the long term. As such they too appear to accord with the theories of Holton (1957). In the long term the A_i firms are comparable with the marginal hierarchical firms of the theory of tertiary activity but, in contradistinction to the firms in that theory, A_i firms can earn subnormal, normal or excess profits in the short term. The B_j business types are comparable to the non-marginal hierarchical firms of the theory of tertiary activity.

The nature of the hypothetical urban place

As the urban place continues to grow the number of different business types A_i that could establish themselves at the centre becomes very great. By the time the radius has increased to $a\sqrt{140.86}$ there will be sufficient population to support business type A_{150} at the centre. With that radius the firms closest to the periphery will be of type A_{47} (Table 7.2, Fig. 7.7) and any other firm A_i ($47 < i < 150$) will only be found at the centre where they can all earn excess profits. Thus out of the 151 (A_0 to A_{150}) A_i business types that could be found in the urban place with radius $a\sqrt{140.86}$, 103 of them could only be found at the centre. The extension of the Lösch model as set out here tends therefore to generate a core-dominated urban place.

    Whereas discussion has been restricted to the consideration of an urban place with radius $a\sqrt{140.86}$ (Fig. 7.7) there is no reason to believe that this represents a limiting case. For the purposes of demonstrating an important characteristic of the model, consideration will be given to the internal structure of the 60 degree sector that includes the second firm of A_{150} (Fig. 7.5). Each of the places in the 60 degree

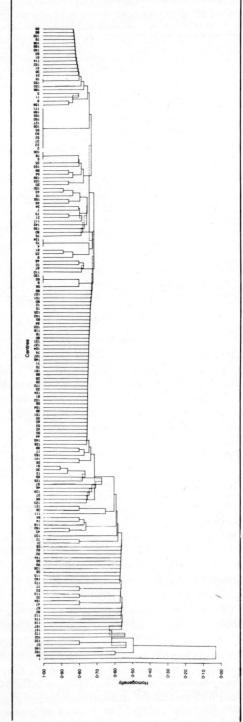

Fig. 7.8   The relationship between shopping centres in the business-rich sector $Y'OC$ of Fig. 7.5 (from Beavon, op. cit., 56, 1974a).

sector of Fig. 7.5 can be described as a shopping centre and the A_i businesses present represent the types of shops. It is clear that there are relatively few identical shopping centres, and that those sets of shopping centres that are identical have relatively few business types. The differences between the shopping centres in this model tend to be subtle, whereas in the Christallerian system the differences between places, or shopping centres as proposed in the theory of tertiary activity, are quite distinct.

Taxonomic comparison

It has been shown that it is possible to use a geotaxonomic measure of similarity for examining both hierarchies and continua of central places (Chapter 4). The results of the application of both the H'_{qm} measure and its associated clustering procedure to the sector $Y'OC$ (the city-rich or business-rich sector)[4] are shown in dendrographic form (Fig. 7.8). Each place in the sector $Y'OC$ can be identified by the set of code numbers shown in Fig. 7.9. The dendrogram tends to suggest that it

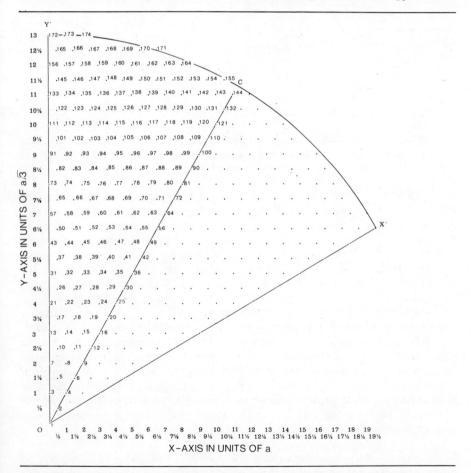

Fig. 7.9 Key to centres in Figs 7.8 and 7.5, and in Figs 7.10 and 7.11 (from Beavon, op. cit., 56, 1974a).

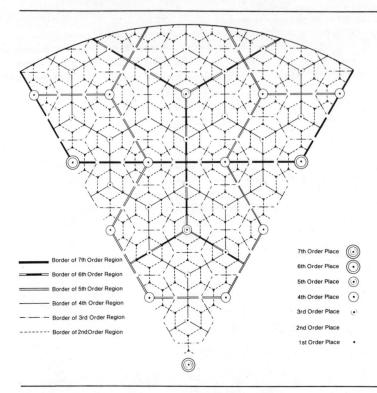

Border of 7th Order Region

Border of 6th Order Region

Border of 5th Order Region

Border of 4th Order Region

— - — - Border of 3rd Order Region

- - - - - - - Border of 2nd Order Region

7th Order Place

6th Order Place

5th Order Place

4th Order Place

3rd Order Place

2nd Order Place

1st Order Place

Fig. 7.10   The K3 system developed with a sector of the same size as shown in Fig. 7.5 with distance between points in the lattice also fixed as *a* (from Beavon, op. cit., 56, 1974a).

is only the set of twelve centres that represent business type A_0 alone, and the centre of the urban place (1) that contains all A_i's (i = 0, 1, 2, . . . 150), that show marked difference from the remaining places. The dendrogram reveals only small successive differences between the remaining 161 shopping centres and suggests a continuum rather than a stepped hierarchy of shopping centres. Accordant results for metropolitan Cape Town have been presented in Chapter 5. Although the central business area of Cape Town was not included in that analysis it is quite reasonable to expect it to have shown a very low level of homogeneity with the extra-CBD centres. The reasons for this are simple. The central business area of Cape Town is considerably larger than any other centre in its metropolitan area (cf. Fig. 5.1) and contains a high proportion of multi-storey business houses. Thus the Cape Town core would contain both a varied set of business types and many businesses (cf. D. H. Davies, 1965; D. H. Davies and Beavon, 1973). For comparison a sector of Christaller's K3 network (Fig. 7.10) has been analysed in the same way[5]. As expected larger numbers of low order places are identical and the differences between the relatively high and relatively low order places quite distinct, as shown on the dendrogram, Fig. 7.11.

In this chapter it has been shown how it is possible to extend the Lösch model of inter-city marketing into a model of the intra-metropolitan commercial system. The model presented is essentially oriented towards the role of the entrepreneur under

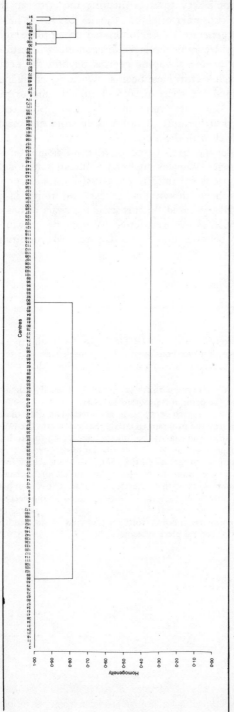

Fig. 7.11 The relationship between places in a sector of a K3 network (Fig. 7.10) corresponding in size with the sector *Y'OC* cf Fig. 7.5 (from Beavon, op. cit., 56, 1974a).

initially restrictive assumptions. Notwithstanding these assumptions it is suggested that the model goes some way towards meeting the criticism that central place theory is normally too consumer oriented (Rowley, 1972). It has been shown how the model will tend to generate a core-dominated urban place unless it is assumed that decentralisation will commence after diseconomies of agglomeration set in. The internal structure of the shopping centres beyond the centre of the urban place, in the business-rich sector, have been shown to resemble more closely a continuum than the stepped hierarchy predicted in both the original central place theory (Christaller, 1933) and its extension as the theory of tertiary activity (Berry and Garrison, 1958c). Furthermore, data available from one major South African city appears to accord well with the model presented here.

The alternative model has been based on a set of assumptions that effectively reduce the vagaries of space. Whereas the Berry and Garrison model is claimed to be independent of assumptions of uniformity of distribution of population and purchasing power, it has been shown that unless uniformity in these respects is assumed the model is falsely based. In this sense the assumptions of the alternative model need not be viewed as over-restrictive. The manner in which the alternative model here proposed behaves under less constrained conditions will now be examined.

Notes

1. This observation has also been made by Saey (1973), and in passing by Lewis (1970).
2. The graphical procedure that was employed is laborious. At present there appears to be no succinct mathematical procedure or computational algorithm that will readily provide this information.
3. The number of firms of each type within a given radius is readily calculated by the addition of a short subroutine to the computer program LOSCH.
4. Only the city-rich or business-rich sector was analysed. The data matrix of 151 x 174 is already extremely large for the program HOMGN that calculates the $(174 \times 174)/2$ items of the H'_{qm} matrix 173 times and makes the linkages according to the linkage algorithm. To analyse the full 60 degree sector $Y'OX''$ in the same manner is at present beyond the reasonable capabilities of the program and the IBM 370/145 machine for which it is written.
5. Strictly speaking it is not possible to compare the models of Christaller and Lösch even when the size of the sectors, as in this case are identical. The reason being that the spacing between places in the Christallerian network is determined on the basis of the outer limit of the range whereas in the Löschian network the concept of the threshold area is employed. Notwithstanding, the comparison does afford a useful view of the dendrographic differences between the two types of central place systems.

Chapter 8

Generalising the intra-urban model

In the previous chapter it was shown how the Lösch model can be interpreted on an intra-urban scale under conditions of isotropism. The intra-urban model so derived is representative of an urban place in which the core area is the dominant business centre. This is certainly the case for South African cities and appears to be the case for the majority of Western cities. The model should be seen not as a deterministic model but rather as a conceptual model of the location of tertiary activities of Western cities and metropolii. In this chapter *some* of the effects of relaxing the isotropic and other assumptions are examined. In so doing an attempt is made to view the model under more general conditions, and to show how the *concepts* embodied in the constrained model remain unaltered even under such generalised conditions.

Relaxation of the constraints and the introduction of some heuristic assumptions

In order to understand more clearly the application of the model to the real world city it is essential that the isotropism be relaxed to take account, for example, of variations in the distribution of purchasing power and population that are associated with real cities. The desire is to develop the model on the minimum of assumptions for both ease of analysis and clarity. However, consideration of such facets as location under conditions of uncertainty, or in areas of varying amounts of purchasing power, are best done initially on the basis of the isotropism provided by the remaining assumptions. Having considered the nature of particular variations their essence can then be noted and synthesised in an attempt to provide a general overall statement of the behaviour of the model.

The effect of changing population density

Population density doubles
Suppose that the urban place had developed to the stage where firms of all business types up to and including A_{47} had spread outwards from the core (Fig. 7.7, p. 114). If with the passage of time population were to increase without a concomitant increase in the area of the urban place, the population density would increase. Suppose that the increase in population density is regular throughout the urban area. From equation 7.2 it is clear that as the density ρ increases so the threshold areas for any set of A_i or B_j firms will decrease in size. It follows that all businesses that had exactly satisfied their threshold requirements prior to an increase in

population density (now designated as A_i^* business types) must now commence earning excess profits. When the population density has doubled, each firm of business type A_i^* will be earning profits equal to twice normal profits and will be satisfying their threshold requirements from a threshold area half the size of the original. Suppose the number of such firms is N^*, then it is possible for an additional N^* firms of type A_i^* to enter the market, and to select a location in such a way that all $2N^*$ firms will again earn only normal profits.

If it is assumed either that consumers patronise, or that the entrepreneurs perceive that consumers patronise, the nearest business, then the only possible equable solution to the location of the additional N^* firms is for each of them to locate immediately adjacent to an existing firm of A_i^*. This will have the effect of halving the original trade areas (Fig. 8.1a and b). This solution to the location

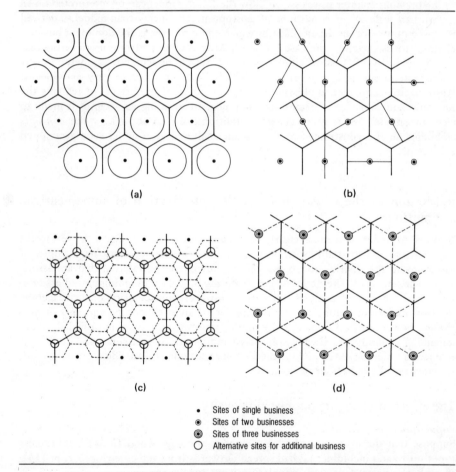

(a)   (b)

(c)   (d)

• Sites of single business
◉ Sites of two businesses
◎ Sites of three businesses
○ Alternative sites for additional business

Fig. 8.1 The location of businesses in response to population increases. (a) Original threshold areas are hexagonal but reduce to circles when population density doubles. (b) Original threshold areas are shared; direction, absence or presence of division lines is immaterial. (c) Threshold areas (dashed lines) one-third the size of the original (solid lines) can provide alternative business locations when population trebles. (d) Original threshold areas are shared; direction, absence or presence of division lines is immaterial (from Beavon, *S. Afr. Geog. J.*, **56**, 1974b).

problem has the effect of increasing the economies of agglomeration for the entrepreneur.

The location problem considered above is essentially one of duopoly and spatial competition. It has been argued that the clustered solution will result in a situation where each firm would be able, at best, to count on the possible patronage of everyone in general (i.e., all the potential customers in the old threshold area) but on no one in particular (Devletoglou, 1965, p. 158). The concept of the *minimum sensible constraint of indifference*, presented by Devletoglou, and the resultant hyperbolic boundaries of the assumed market areas has a certain heuristic appeal. Certainly it implies that a single fixed value of a threshold is not acceptable. Nonetheless, it could reasonably be expected that entrepreneurs will make allowance for the necessary additional population, that might be required to offset such a sharing of a market, when setting their threshold requirements. Moreover it is reasonable to expect that threshold requirements are likely to be set within upper and lower estimates for a set of identical businesses and not at some exact amount. This would also be in accordance with ideas expressed by Garner (1966) (cf. Chapter 2). Notwithstanding, for pedogogic purposes an exact amount is normally assumed and employed in theoretical arguments.

The agglomeration of tertiary activities appears to be supported by the literature concerned with the role of uncertainty in location decisions. It has been suggested that most human decision making, at both the individual and organisational level, is concerned only with the selection of a *satisfactory* alternative. Only in exceptional cases are optimal alternatives considered (March and Simon, 1958, pp. 140–1; Hamilton, 1967, pp. 364–8). The important consideration for profits over long periods of time under uncertainty is that the firm stays in business. Firms realise that their profits depend in part on the location of later sellers and consumers and they try to secure a location that will be reasonably good. As such they tend to choose locations that will allow them to stay in business no matter what other firms decide (Webber, 1972, p. 109) and tend therefore to select locations in existing shopping centres, as *inter alia* such locations enhance the ease with which competitive firms can realise the need for, and affect adjustments in prices and stock varieties. Certainly the principles of cumulative attraction and compatibility (Nelson, 1958) would tend to enhance the attraction of existing shopping centres and so generate agglomeration economies. Furthermore, economies of agglomeration would normally increase the degree of concentration within an urban system (Webber, 1972, pp. 275 and 281). Although the arguments of uncertainty presented by Webber are essentially concerned with secondary activity they appear general enough to be applicable to the tertiary sector as well. Certainly the concentration of fairly large numbers of businesses in a relatively small number of shopping centres in urban areas bears witness to tertiary agglomeration.

Zoning regulations in an urban area can further enhance the agglomeration tendency. Zoning for business is normally introduced at some stage of urban growth for any large urban place and thereby limits the degree of business dispersal. In addition the application for a rezoning of a site for business purposes is more likely to succeed if such a site is already adjacent to an existing business area, as opposed to a lone site in an otherwise residential area. A decision that again contributes to agglomeration.

Population density trebles
Having discussed the probable location decision for new firms based on a doubling

of population density, consideration can be given to the case where population density increases rapidly by a factor of three. In such a case threshold areas would be only a third of their original size, and for the N^* firms so effected it would be possible for an additional $2N^*$ new firms to enter the market. In this case two different solutions are possible. If the new firms took up interstitial positions between the existing firms (Fig. 8.1c), all A_i^* firms would be equidistant from their nearest competing neighbour, all would be capable of earning normal profits and all would have threshold areas one-third the size of their original. Such a solution would tend to reduce the aggregate travel by consumers, but certainly represents an invasion of the relative privacy of the residential areas. The comparative social costs of this solution and the alternative solution, where two of the additional $2N^*$ firms locate immediately adjacent to each A_i^* firm in existing shopping centres, must be considered (Fig. 8.1d). The latter solution offers increased economies of agglomeration for the entrepreneur and minimises the intrusion of business activity into residential areas, while at the same time ensuring that each firm has the opportunity of satisfying its threshold requirements from equal sized threshold areas (Fig. 8.1d).

It is unlikely that densities of population would increase so rapidly as to preclude the location of new firms at a stage when the density was equal to, or approaching, a figure twice as high as that which originally prevailed. As the most likely solution at that intermediate stage would have been one that favoured agglomeration of activities in existing centres, such a pattern is likely to persist in the long run as densities continue to increase.

Population density decreases
If the population density of the urban place decreases the effect is essentially the converse of the cases just considered. With a uniform decrease in density, and in accordance with the set of equations 7.1 to 7.3 as derived from the set of assumptions (in Chapter 7), threshold areas must necessarily increase in size. Given a finite urban area it follows that there will now be insufficient population to support all existing firms. Suppose that the density were decreased rapidly throughout the urban area by a factor of two. Theoretically one out of every two firms of the same type located in the same shopping centre would have to close down. In fact it is more likely that both such businesses would be forced to close down although one of them might be resuscitated, be it under the same or new management. The principles of cumulative attraction and compatibility assist in assuring the success of a new firm, located in the same shopping centre as an original firm, when densities are increased. However, when densities decrease these same principles will tend to split the remaining population between the two firms, thus ensuring that both close down unless by a process of collusion one closes down immediately. If both firms are forced to close it is possible that one might re-open under the new equilibrium conditions. The theoretical approach set out here in terms of the present intra-urban model appears to accord well with the process underlying the incidence of economic blight as, for example, described in Chicago (Berry, 1963).

In considering the constrained intra-urban model under these more general circumstances allowance can readily be made for the duplication of business types in shopping centres central to zones of increasing population density. Likewise allowance can be made for the demise of duplicated business types under conditions of declining density. The intra-urban model appears capable of the type of modification suggested. The type of business A_i that is capable of locating at any point so that it will earn at least normal profits in the long run can be calculated.

This can be done by comparing the maximum threshold area that can be supported with that which would be necessary for a particular A_i business, at a particular shopping centre, that is central to a part of the city that is experiencing a change in population.

The effects of relaxing the constraints on population density are similar to those that will result from the relaxation of constraints that imply homogeneous distribution of income.

Effect of varying income

Under the assumption of isotropism the income of all individuals (or households) is implied to be equal. Hence it has been possible, under the conditions of assumed equal population density, to equate not only an increase in density with an increase in population, but with concomitant increases in sales by A_i firms and a decrease in $_a t_i$ threshold areas. If both individual (or household) incomes and the distribution of income groups is allowed to vary the pattern already presented changes.

Let the income for any individual (or household) l be $\bar{c}_l$. The threshold area of a particular firm is expressed by equation 7.2. If an increase in income for a particular area j of the urban place results from an income multiplier so that income is eventually doubled, then the total income I_j of that j area, having L individuals, is given by

$$I_j = 2 \sum_{l=1}^{L} \bar{c}_l \tag{8.1}$$

The conclusion could be drawn that:

$$_a t_i = (_A n_i / \rho) / (I_j / C) \tag{8.2}$$

where

$$C = \sum_{l=1}^{L} \bar{c}_l \tag{8.3}$$

The implication of equation 8.2 is that if the threshold area for business type A_i is $_a t_i$ when income is I, if income as a result of a multiplier effect is *increased* by a factor f then the threshold area is *decreased* by the same factor. This is an erroneous argument in general, although it may hold in certain cases. It is erroneous because an increase in income does not necessarily mean a proportionate amount will be spent across all types of commodities. Whereas an increase of income in a low-income area may result in more money being spent on food items, the same increase in a high-income area is unlikely to result in any additional increase in the demand for food. The amount of additional expenditure upon any commodity will be a function of the income elasticity of demand for that commodity in different parts of the urban place.

In essence an increase in income in a part of the urban place can result in the advent of a new firm A_k even though a firm of A_k might not yet have appeared in the core area. The addition of new commodities that are themselves associated with purchases by higher income groups in existing firms is also a possibility. The location of a new firm A_k resulting from income changes will affect the location of further businesses of the same type.

A decline in income may lead to commercial blight and/or to firms going out of business, as in the case of declining population density. In this case declining firms may be rehabilitated or new and different types might appear. This would probably be the case if the decline in incomes was not accompanied by population change (Lipsey, 1966, p. 194n).

Random location of new firms

In the constrained model it is assumed that firms with threshold areas $_a t_i$ ($i = 0, 1, 2, 3, \ldots$) will successively commence operations at the centre of the urban place. Furthermore, it is implied by assumptions 4 and 5 that all firms of type A_i will gradually diffuse outward from the centre of the urban place. As now shown, higher income levels in a part of the urban place might provide the basis for the establishment of a particular type of business that cannot be supported in other parts of the urban area outside of the core. It is possible that the appearance of such a firm might take place prior to the steady diffusion of the same type of firm from the centre. This introduces the possibility of such a firm being located randomly relative to the potential sites defined in accordance with assumptions 4 and 5. The effects of random location by a firm or firms in the suburbs is best done by relaxing assumptions 3 and 4 thereby permitting a random location to be chosen. Having made such a choice all the assumptions with the exception of assumption 5 are again considered to be operative. The resultant development of the market system can now be studied.

Consider a firm $A_{k,1}$ that is located at the centre of the urban place, and a second firm $A_{k,2}$ that is located in accordance with assumptions 4, 5 and 6. The location of these two firms determines the potential sites for further A_k firms from among the set of all potential business sites. Purely for reference purposes the latter set are indicated as defined by $A_{0,1}$ and $A_{0,2}$ as if assumption 5 had initially been operative (Fig. 8.2).

Suppose that it is possible as a result of relatively high incomes in the general area D, E, F, G (Fig. 8.2) for a firm $A'_{k,1}$ to establish itself and earn at least normal profits. The firm $A'_{k,1}$ selects its location without adherence to assumptions 4 and 5 and thus effectively locates randomly with respect to the firms of the same type $A_{k,1}$ and $A_{k,2}$, already located at and near the centre of the urban place. Let the location of $A'_{k,1}$ be as shown in Fig. 8.2. Now in accordance with assumption 4, all assumptions now being re-applied, a second firm $A'_{k,2}$ locates in the general area D, E, F, G and by so doing establishes a set of potential sites for all $A'_{k,i}$ firms. Similarly, let a firm $A''_{k,1}$ select a random location where it earns at least normal profits. Following the selection of a location for the firm $A''_{k,2}$, in accordance with assumption 4, a set of potential sites for all $A''_{k,i}$ firms is determined. Let the development of further firms now take place within the three systems of A_k-type firms in accordance with the set of assumptions. In terms of assumption 4 the threshold areas of all the A_k-type firms (i.e., all A_k, A'_k and A''_k) have been shown as hexagons in Fig. 8.2.

Whereas all the trade areas shown in Fig. 8.2 are necessarily of equal size, the random selection of locations for $A'_{k,1}$ and $A''_{k,1}$ has, in the case shown, precluded the nets of hexagonal trade areas centred on these firms from being, or eventually being, contiguous throughout the urban area. As shown the hexagonal trade areas form three sets of equal area contiguous hexagonal networks that are not contiguous between sets. The shaded areas (Fig. 8.2) represent parts of the urban place that may be served by A_k firms of either the A'_k, A''_k or A_k networks. The shaded

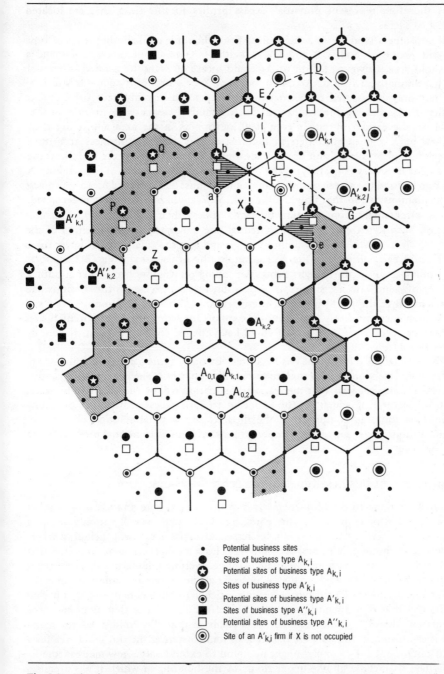

- •   Potential business sites
- ●   Sites of business type $A_{k,i}$
- ✪   Potential sites of business type $A_{k,i}$
- ◉   Sites of business type $A'_{k,i}$
- ⊙   Potential sites of business type $A'_{k,i}$
- ■   Sites of business type $A''_{k,i}$
- □   Potential sites of business type $A''_{k,i}$
- ◉   Site of an $A'_{k,i}$ firm if X is not occupied

Fig. 8.2 The development about randomly chosen business sites. Two sites $A'_{k,1}$ and $A''_{k,1}$ are chosen randomly with respect to potential sites generated by the location of $A_{k,1}$ and $A_{k,2}$ in accordance with the assumptions stated in the text. Shaded areas represent areas of potential excess profits for existing businesses. It is assumed that a business will be established at Z (from Beavon, op. cit., 56, 1974b).

areas therefore represent potential excess profits for the firms that are located closest to them.

If consumers tend to visit the nearest firm, then it is unlikely that firms of type A_k will locate at points P and Q, as neither of these points can command a threshold area. However, a firm of A_k could locate at Z and be assured of normal profits. Similarly, a firm of A_k could locate at X or a firm of A_k' could locate at Y and not only be assured of normal profits but could possibly earn some excess profits. If A_k and A_k' firms locate at *both* X and Y respectively, normal profits could not be earned by either even if all customers in the area a, b, c did their business at X and all customers in the area d, e, f did their business at Y, thus compensating for the division of the trade areas of X and Y about the line cd. As the conditions necessary for satisfying the normal profits requirement of firms at both X and Y go beyond the present set of assumptions, it must be concluded for the purposes of this demonstration that only a firm at X or Y could be reasonably entertained.

The effect of random location by firms, unless their choice or selection of a location accords exactly with the potential site generated by the location of the first two firms according to assumptions 3, 4, and 5, is the emergence of fewer firms than could earn normal profits. For example, the urban area in Fig. 8.2 supports only thirty-seven or thirty-eight firms (depending on whether firms exist at both X and Y) of which twenty-six are in a position to earn excess profits. If firms had only located at the set of potential sites, determined by the locations of $A_{k,1}$ and $A_{k,2}$, then forty-six firms (indicated by symbols for *both* actual and potential sites of business type $A_{k,i}$ in Fig. 8.2) could have opened for business but made only normal profits.

The real world selection of business sites obviously bears a closer resemblance to the random selection process than to the idealised pattern. The generalised situation discussed above suggests that the real world situation will be characterised by fewer A_i firms, several of which can be expected to earn excess profits even over long periods of time, as compared to the theoretically optimal solution of the constrained model where more firms operate but are limited to normal profits only in the long run.

Duplication of business types in the central business core

As firms continue to establish themselves in the central core an increasing number of persons will be employed in the core area. These persons will not only be those employed by tertiary retailers, wholesalers, and offices, but will include workers associated with the public and government (at least local government) activities that operate in the core. With an essentially captive daytime population the core takes on the attributes of a residential area, in so far as the working population can make use of the businesses (retail businesses in particular) of the core during that period of the day that they spend in the core. The effect is similar to that of an increased population density in the suburbs. The result is that threshold areas for many activities located in the core are reduced. In some instances the threshold area for a small restaurant, for example, might be found to extend only a few metres from its door, but to include all the upper floors of the building in which it has premises (the threshold area in this case might be more appropriately described as a threshold volume). As a result yet another small restaurant, for all intents and purposes identical, will be able to enter the market and earn at least normal profits located at the foot of another office block, albeit less than 100 metres away from the first. On this basis new firms, particularly those with low to middle order threshold requirements, can enter the market and multiply in the core area of the urban place.

The duplication of businesses in the core is facilitated not only by the captive daytime working population, but is further enhanced by the attraction of consumers to high-threshold firms that are located in the core. Consumers attracted to the latter businesses may for the sake of convenience spend money (make purchases) at other businesses in the core.

The core can be regarded as representative of all businesses in the urban place as a whole. It is generally accepted that there is a zonal structure of the core where businesses are located relative to the peak land value site according to their ability to pay rent. Given these two observations it is suggested that the intra-urban model can be generalised to *represent* this situation by the simple process of viewing the graphic representation of the model (e.g. Fig. 7.7, p. 114), or an appropriate part of it, as the core area itself[1].

A corollary of the increased daytime population in the core area is the relative decrease in the population of the suburban areas. The net result is that sales during the week and the main part of the day will be low in the suburban areas but high at the end of the day and at the weekend. Effectively this situation might increase the threshold requirement, or threshold estimates by the entrepreneur for items in the suburban shopping centres. The model appears capable of handling such a situation if it is approached in a manner similar to that employed in considering the random location of firms. Obviously with a variation in the size of thresholds, as proposed here, a mismatch of threshold areas *must* occur. The result will be a reduction in the number of firms, relative to an optimum number under conditions of equilibrium, and an increase in the excess profits for some of the firms.

Effects of relaxed assumptions on the shape of threshold areas

Given the conditions of homogeneity inherent in the set of original assumptions, networks of regular hexagonal threshold areas of discrete size are characteristic of each A_i business type that spreads outwards from the core. Consideration must be given to the effect that a relaxation of the isotropism would have on such regular hexagon areas. For example, consider the effects that a non-uniform density of population would have on the shape of the hexagon trade areas for a business type A_i if all the other assumptions in the set of assumptions are held constant.

The problem posed has been viewed as one of a class of problems requiring the development of a map projection, more aptly a map transformation, that would enable a particular real world pattern to be viewed as a spatially distorted pattern of its theoretical counterpart (Tobler, 1963, 1970).

In order to overcome the problems encountered in the earlier map transformation procedure (Tobler, 1970) a fresh attempt has recently been made to solve the problems of map transformations of central place point patterns in areas of variable population density (Rushton, 1972). An example of such transformations is shown in Figs 8.3 and 8.4 where population densities are allowed to vary from a plane homogeneous surface (Fig. 8.3) through increasingly complex surface forms (Fig. 8.4a to d). Notwithstanding the desire to retain the original relationships between supply points and the boundaries of the threshold area, Rushton found it became necessary to state the problem as one of determining the location of supply points such that in the area surrounding each supply point *approximately* equal amounts

Fig. 8.3   The location of business sites on an isotropic plane. Each business site is surrounded by a hexagonal threshold area that encloses identical populations.

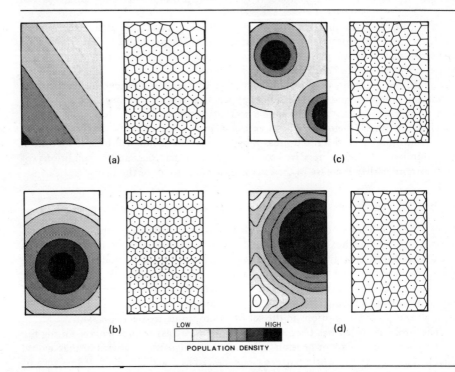

Fig. 8.4   Effects of varying population density on the shape of threshold areas. The shape of the hexagons (Fig. 8.3) becomes increasingly distorted as population density is allowed to depart from the isotropic distribution and to assume more complicated patterns (a, b, c, d) (after Rushton, *Reg. Sci. Ass. Pap.*, **28**, 1972).

of demand (i.e., population, assuming each person has the same demand) corresponding to a given *threshold demand* will exist. The reason for introducing the concept of *approximate areas* and by implication *approximate distance* to supply points is that it is not possible to simultaneously impose the constraint of equal capacity at each supply point *and* the constraint that the population be so demarcated by threshold boundaries that the aggregate distance, *ceteris paribus*,

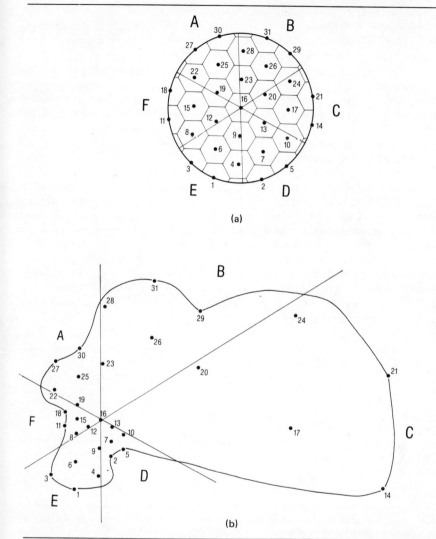

Fig. 8.5   Relative location of business sites under varying conditions of population density. (a) Business sites evenly distributed under general conditions of isotropism. (b) Business sites evenly distributed under conditions of sectoral isotropism. Sectors A and E have unit density ρ, sectors B, C, D, and F have densities $\rho/4$, $\rho/10$, 4ρ, and 4ρ respectively (from Beavon, op. cit., 56, 1974b).

remain equal to that experienced when population density is uniform in all directions about the supply point.

If the isotropism is relaxed, not only with respect to population density but simultaneously with respect to incomes and ease of movement, the difficulty of drawing hexagonal boundaries even on an approximate basis will be considerably increased. For example, given thirty-one business sites and a homogeneous distribution of population, an equilibrium of supply is possible (Fig. 8.5). Let the relative population densities of the sectors B, C, D, E, and F (in Fig. 8.5a) change such that they become 0.25, 0.10, 4.0, 1.0, and 4.0 times the density respectively of the unaltered sector A. Whereas it is easy to plot the new locations of the shopping centres relative to each other (Fig. 8.5b), it is not possible to retain the hexagons or even the *hexagonality* of the threshold areas as originally portrayed in Fig. 8.5a. Only by allowing the threshold areas to be drawn as irregular polygons can an approximate set of threshold areas again be demarcated.

It appears inevitable that the original hexagonal boundaries of the threshold areas of the intra-urban model must eventually become curvilinear polygons in all but the simplest generalisations. In this context the criticism, that transformed hexagonal market areas do not correspond with the theories or empirical findings of market area analysis (Rushton, 1972, p. 113), must be viewed with caution. A trade area and a threshold area can only be equated if consumer demand and behaviour are identical for all persons. Given from random sampling that there is a probability p_i that an individual will purchase an item i in a given time period, it is possible to calculate threshold area and threshold population that will be required by the firm dealing in that commodity if the threshold sales level for the firm is known (equations 7.1 to 7.3). However, the actual distribution of the persons who purchase item i need not be even. Thus for three identical threshold areas three different distributions of actual consumers could be possible (Fig. 8.6). Furthermore the interpretations of the polygons, even if they be curvilinear after transformation, can only be made if the variations in accessibility that have been entered, or allowed to enter the situation, are recognised.

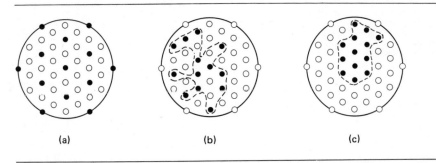

(a)   (b)   (c)

Fig. 8.6 Distribution of customers within a threshold area. The circle demarcates a threshold area. Customers (black dots) may be (a) evenly distributed, (b) scattered, (c) clustered within the population (open dots) enclosed by the threshold area. The shape of the resultant market areas is indicated by dashed lines. Only in case (a) is the market area boundary coincident with the boundary of the threshold area (from Beavon, op. cit., 56, 1974b).

Operation of A_i businesses under changing cost functions

The operation of A_i businesses in the constrained model accords with the observation that over time the urban system demonstrates a trend towards an optimal condition in which excess profits are non-existent (Berry and Garrison, 1958b). The operation of the B_j firms is, however, in accordance with Lösch's (1954) view of a marketing system where the earning of at least small amounts of excess profits is the norm for the majority of business types.

It appears appropriate in the interests of attempting to generalise the model to consider the operation of firms *within the model* under conditions of changing cost functions. This can be achieved by recourse to basic economic principles. In this way the model can be shown to represent closely the real spatial organisation of economic activities. An organisation that has been described as the product of both economic and non-economic forces, comprising establishments whose locations either permit varying degrees of profit making, or prohibit the earning of excess profits over long periods of time, but very rarely allowing for profit maximisation (Pred, 1966). It will be shown that by relaxing the assumption of the constrained model relating to constant cost functions (assumption number 8), it becomes *possible* for the A_i firms in the model to earn relative and varying amounts of excess profits over long periods of time, regardless of their location relative to other A_i firms[2]. It also becomes possible for B_j firms to increase their profit margins.

The firms of business types A_i and B_j are not necessarily businesses dealing only in single commodities. On the contrary, such firms are more likely to be multi-product businesses. For the argument that follows it is appropriate to describe the threshold requirements of such firms in terms of their threshold *sales*. Furthermore prices of commodities can either be described as the price of a single commodity, or the price of an average 'bundle' of commodities representing a sale from a multi-product firm.

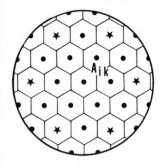

Fig. 8.7   Distribution of a set of A_i businesses: all firms with the exception of the outer twelve are assumed to earn normal profits, although the firms indicated by the stars should be earning small excess profits (from Beavon, *S. Afr. Geog. J.*, **58**, 1976).

Consider the set of A_i firms established under the set of fourteen assumptions that govern the constrained model. Although six of the inner firms (Fig. 8.7) can earn small amounts of excess profits, for ease of argument, it will be assumed that they too only earn normal profits as do all other inner firms. Given that threshold sales requirements are Q commodities per firm where the metropolitan price, P_M, is determined by the prevailing average revenue curve (AR_1, Fig. 8.8). The average revenue curves of each of the nineteen inner firms in the example must be tangential to their average short run cost curves[3] as shown in Fig. 8.8.

Suppose firm $A_{i,k}$ (Fig. 8.7), by exacting internal economies, is able to reduce its average costs by an amount $M-N$. By maintaining the price of the commodity at P_M the demand curve remains unaltered, but the firm $A_{i,k}$ now earns profits equal to the rectangle $WXMN$ in Fig. 8.9. This will attract competitors and it is assumed now that firm $A_{i,j}$ locates at the same position in space. Under this condition the

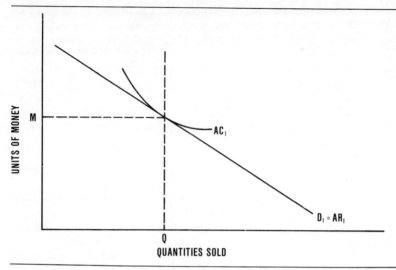

Fig. 8.8   The relationship between the average short-run cost curve and the revenue curve for an A_i firm earning normal profits (from Beavon, op. cit., **58**, 1976).

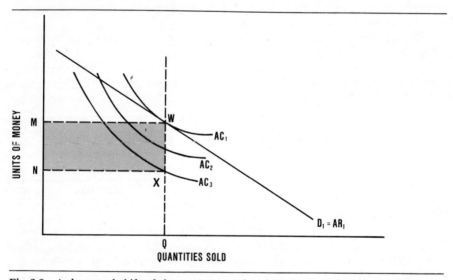

Fig. 8.9   A downward shift of the average cost function allows relative excess profits to be earned. When average costs drop from AC_1 to AC_3 the profits are given by the rectangle *WXMN* (from Beavon, op. cit., **58**, 1976).

demand curves for the two individual firms will shift from D_1 to D_2, and the quantity of commodities sold by each firm will be half that sold by $A_{i,k}$ prior to the advent of $A_{i,j}$. Nevertheless, it will be possible for firm $A_{i,k}$ to continue earning at least normal profits provided that the average cost curve is tangential to or above the average revenue curve (Fig. 8.10, where the marginal situation is shown). This implies that efficient firms, if able to reduce their average costs from say AC_1 to AC_3 (Fig. 8.9), will remain in business on a normal profit basis although the

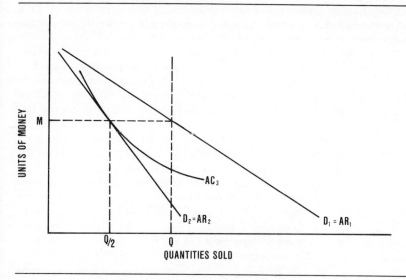

Fig. 8.10   Entry of a second firm $A_{i,j}$ is assumed to halve the demand and the average revenue curve shifts from AR_1 to AR_2 (from Beavon, op. cit., **58**, 1976).

quantity of commodities they sell is reduced. The threshold requirements of such firms can now be regarded as altered. It follows that the new firm $A_{i,j}$ will also be able to earn normal profits *provided* it is able to operate at the lower average costs achieved by the firm $A_{i,k}$. If the new firm $A_{i,j}$ operates on a cost curve higher than AC_3 then it will be forced out of business and the firm $A_{i,k}$ can again revert to earning excess profits.

Whereas it may be possible for a firm $A_{i,k}$ to reduce its average costs over time and thus assure itself of earning excess profits it is unlikely that a new firm $A_{i,j}$ will be able to compete at the same average costs from the outset of its operation (Parr and Denike, 1970, pp. 579–80), although this may be the case if the new firm is part of a chain organisation. In practice it could be expected that new firms will enter the market under the conditions described but that in many instances either they, the existing firm or both will be forced out of business. In the latter case a single A_i firm could enter the market and commence operations on the same basis as other A_i firms.

Contained in the above discussion is the assumption that purchasing power, population density, socio-economic status, etc., remain constant in the threshold area of the firm $A_{i,k}$ during the period of possible competition. Under the relaxed assumption that A_i firms operate under changing cost functions, the earning of excess profits becomes possible even over long periods of time for A_i firms. Similarly the earning of greater amounts of excess profits can become possible for the B_j firms in the model. The introduction of the relaxed assumption relating to cost functions does not invalidate the model. The earning of normal, subnormal and excess profits remains possible for A_i firms in the short run as in the case of the fully constrained model. By allowing A_i firms to earn excess profits even over long periods of time the model remains structurally the same but the profit situation is made more realistic and the overall similarity between the organisation of firms in the model with those of the real world as described by Pred (1966) is enhanced.

Demands for particular types of businesses reflecting a variety of quantities and qualities of commodities vary according to the compounded distribution of population, incomes, and social status. The whole pattern is further influenced by the varying nature of the topography and transportation lines. As consumer behaviour is uncertain, it is reasonable to suppose that entrepreneurs operating under conditions of uncertainty will tend to set higher threshold levels than would be the case if certainty existed. In order to offset the uncertainty of consumer behaviour an entrepreneur will select his location more cautiously and central to a larger area than might be necessary. Given that the skill of each entrepreneur in estimating his thresholds will vary, it follows that the threshold estimates for a particular business type will vary from low to high estimates. Similarly the range or outer limit of the business will have high and low estimates. As the population of an urban place grows, the central area will provide a location for a variety of different types and numbers of business. The success of each business will depend *inter alia* on the acumen and skill of the entrepreneur in assessing his thresholds and ranges, relative to the growing population, competitive businesses and in the management of his business. As the urban place grows outwards access to the central area becomes more difficult in terms of time, effort and cost. Eventually firms will select locations to reach the outlying or suburban population more efficiently. Depending on the pattern of sites selected, so pools of relatively unserved population or untapped purchasing power will emerge. Firms well placed in terms of their range limits will have the opportunity of greater overall success in business, whether this be measured merely by ability to stay in business or by making excess profits. Firms in competition with one another that are unable to locate in the same shopping centres because of insufficient threshold population will choose alternative locations relative to other such firms. Firms that are not in competition with other firms, for the satisfaction of their threshold requirements, will nest within the threshold areas of those firms that have satisfied higher threshold requirements. Given the varied nature of accessibility and socio-economic status of the city, it follows that the larger the agglomeration of businesses in a shopping centre the lower is the probability that any two centres will be identical in terms of both number and type of business. For a large metropolitan city with many shopping centres a continuum rather than a stepped hierarchy will therefore be more characteristic.

The key to interpreting the intra-metropolitan model, presented in this book, under general circumstances is the variable set of concepts that can be applied to the value of the distance *a* between any two business sites. It must be seen to represent *inter alia* physical, social, cost, and economic distance, either separately or in combination. Thus the generalised model is capable of taking many forms each depending upon the circumstances under which the constrained model is considered.

Notes

1. Each 'dot' on the diagram of the constrained model may represent one or more city blocks and the distance *a* assumes a role as will be discussed at the end of this chapter.
2. The discussion that follows is similar to that presented by Denike and Parr (1970) and Parr and Denike (1970) when considering *inter-urban* relationships.
3. For convenience the term average short run costs will be referred to simply as average costs hereafter.

Chapter 9

Conclusions

The previous chapters have shown that the intra-urban location of shopping centres can be explained either by the use of Christaller's central place theory, as has been done by Berry and Garrison in their theory of tertiary activity, or by the use of Lösch's concepts of market areas as has been attempted in this study. Resulting from a review of the ideas and models of Christaller, Berry and Garrison, and Lösch together with the available techniques for evaluating the validity of these models, an alternative conceptual model of the location of intra-metropolitan tertiary activity has been presented in this book. In so doing a critical reassessment has been made of existing theories and techniques associated with them. In passing a number of conclusions have been drawn. It appears desirable to express them in this chapter in as succinct a fashion as possible. In considering the conclusions that are so set out below it is essential to consider them within the context of the fuller arguments that have in turn been set out in detail in the preceding chapters. To consider the conclusions set out below outside of the context of the preceding chapters would be foolhardy.

The main conclusions can now be summarised as follows:

Christaller's central place system

1.1 Contrary to the supposition that an isotropic plane is required for the development of the central place system, it has been shown that the system can be developed using a transportation plane across which population is regularly but unevenly distributed. This allows threshold requirements to be met from small areas about large central places.

1.2 Likewise Christaller did not assume an equilateral lattice of places. The location of the central places emerge as part of the deductive approach that was employed.

1.3 Elaborating on Christaller's imprecise statement of the relationship between the threshold and the outer range of a commodity, it is shown that excess profits are available to businesses throughout the system. The amount of profit is dependent upon the exact relationship that exists between threshold and range.

1.4 The popularly held assumption that the extent of the threshold area bears a constant proportional relationship to the outer limit of the range of a commodity is falsely based and is in conflict with the uneven distribution of population assumed by Christaller.

1.5 The highest order commodity offered from a central place is not necessarily determined by the range of the region of that central place.

The development of the theory of tertiary activity

2.1 Careful review of the literature relating to the development and testing of the theory of tertiary activity suggests that, in the past, the results of empirical studies were influenced by the importance attached to central place theory and its prediction of a stepped hierarchy.

2.2 The finding, that a stepped hierarchy of central places developed on the basis of threshold levels is only possible if an even distribution of population or purchasing power is assumed to occur in the interstitial areas between places of the same order, has been confirmed.

2.3 Despite the theory of tertiary activity being falsely based, the finding that Christaller's stepped hierarchical system is based on a regular but uneven distribution of population provides the basis for concluding that a stepped hierarchy can be argued for a system of tertiary activities other than on an isotropic surface.

2.4 On the basis of behavioural aspects that consumers do not necessarily visit the nearest shopping centre, Rushton has shown that a central place system that yields a continuum of intra-urban central places is possible.

2.5 On the basis of structural aspects the differential effects of commercial blight have been shown to have an influence on the recognition of hierarchical groups.

2.6 The structural component of the theory of tertiary activity must be developed to take into account the existence of intra-urban continua of shopping centres.

Classification of intra-urban hierarchies

3.1 Traditional two-parameter and centrality index methods of distinguishing hierarchies have been shown to be deficient in their practical application. The recognition of so-called clear breaks in data sets has been found to be questionable.

3.2 Difficulties of normalising data and subsequent difficulties in interpretation of analytical results suggests the need for a multivariate technique other than that of the factor analytic type.

3.3 The frequency modulated relative homogeneity function and its associated average member linkage procedure has been shown to be useful in determining the nature of urban hierarchies.

Derivation of the Löschian system of market areas

4.1 Lösch's area numbers provide a nomenclature for identifying successively larger hexagonal market areas that form the base for networks of such market areas. Only hexagons with a size such that the centres of hexagons in their network coincide with points in Lösch's basic lattice are allocated an area number.

4.2 Kanzig's method for calculating the number of points enclosed by each hexagonal market area, and its associated area number has been found to be incorrect as published. A corrected set of equations has been developed.

4.3 Application of these corrected equations does not generate the complete Löschian system owing to their failure to recognise the possibility of alternative locations for the centre of a particular market area (i.e., points equidistant from the metropolis can be centres for the same market area).

4.4 The city rich and city-poor sectors distinction is a constraint upon the development of the system and not a result of the 'rotation' of the networks.

4.5 The centres of market areas are located at points in the basic lattice successively, from the smallest market area upwards. A centre of a particular market area that has alternative locations must be located at that alternative that is already the centre for the largest number of market area centres that have previously been assigned. When both alternatives are centres for the same number of different market areas, the centre in question is located at that alternative that is the centre for the largest market area that has been assigned at the time.

4.6 Lösch shows only the locations of market area centres for fifty-five superimposed networks of market areas. In this study the complete system of 150 superimposed networks of market areas has been developed, tabulated and shown diagrammatically. A simplified procedure for deriving the centres of market areas has also been provided.

4.7 There is no justification for equating two places in a hierarchy merely because they are both the centre for the same total number of market areas. Each market area with a different area number is a different size and is therefore representative of an activity that requires a threshold area of that size. Activities can be distinguished by their threshold requirements. It is therefore essential to distinguish between two places by the type of market centres they are and not simply by the number of market areas centred on them. This is the key to developing the intra-metropolitan model of the location of tertiary activity.

The constrained model of the location of intra-metropolitan tertiary activity

5.1 A distinction is made between two types of businesses, those that earn normal profits in the long run and those that earn excess profits over a long period of time. These businesses correspond with the marginal hierarchical and non-marginal hierarchical firms respectively of the theory of tertiary activity.

5.2 The model represents a core-dominated urban place.

5.3 As the urban place represented by the model is allowed to grow the smallest business type spreads outwards most rapidly from the core and determines the location of future business sites. Thus the model is developed from the smallest business type upwards, in contrast to the models of both Christaller and Berry and Garrison which are developed from the highest order business type downwards.

5.4 The model allows firms to pre-empt locations to the possible profit of the entrepreneur, and in the short run the earning of subnormal, normal or excess profits is possible.

5.5 The model is based upon a distinction between threshold sales, threshold population and threshold area.

5.6 In the model, metropolii develop business-rich and business-poor sectors analagous to the city-rich and city-poor sectors of the original inter-city model of Lösch.

5.7 The model predicts a shopping centre continuum in accordance with observations.

5.8 The constrained intra-metropolitan model of the location of tertiary activity presents a more dynamic conceptual view of the real city and one structurally more in accord with reality than the Berry–Garrison model.

The unconstrained model

6.1 Increases in population density and income lead to duplication of some business types and the possible advent of new types. This in turn leads to increased agglomeration in existing shopping centres.

6.2 Decrease in the above parameters leads to the demise of the existing businesses and a possible change in the types of businesses located in existing shopping centres.

6.3 The effects of random location of firms relative to other firms of the same type shows that excess profits are increased for some firms. However, fewer firms than the maximum number in the constrained model will be able to enter the market successfully.

6.4 As the core area of the unconstrained model develops, so it will become possible for business types to be duplicated in the core. Such is not permitted by the constraints. However, in the unconstrained model replication of business locations normally associated with the constrained model can develop *within* the core area.

6.5 The relaxation that costs are constant for identical types of businesses allows successful businesses to increase their profits. Thus all businesses may earn excess profits over long periods of time. Unsuccessful businesses will be forced out of the market and marginally successful firms will earn only normal profits. New firms are encouraged to enter the market on a competitive basis.

6.6 Under the relaxed constraints the hexagonal shape of the threshold areas about firms must necessarily become distorted even to the extent of becoming un-recognisable. It is essential to distinguish between the shape of a threshold area and the shape of a market area; the two will no longer by synonymous. The unconstrained model is necessarily non-graphical in constradistinction to the constrained model.

6.7 The key to the understanding of the unconstrained model and its application to the real city is the varying set of concepts that can be applied to the distances that separate shopping centres from one another.

6.8 There is no *a priori* basis for expecting the relaxation of the constraints to create a change from a continuum of shopping centres to a stepped hierarchy of shopping centres.

The material presented in Chapter 5 indicated that in Cape Town there is a continuum of shopping centres and not a stepped, or even clear-cut, hierarchy for the city as a whole. The model that has been presented here based essentially on the ideas of Lösch must be tested at the empirical level in other cities. The dearth of detailed documentary evidence will always preclude an in-depth study that traces the development over time of a South African metropolis and assesses it against the model. However, it is possible that documentary evidence in other parts of the world may allow such studies to be conducted. The structural elements of the alternative model can be readily tested using the geotaxonomic approach that has been discussed. In addition the ideas on the relationships between probability of purchases being made, threshold sales, threshold populations, and threshold areas should provide the basis for empirical studies designed to test aspects of what has been presented in this book. Only by such and other studies can it be assessed whether the alternative model presented here is an improvement on what has gone before.

In conclusion it can be said that in this book Christaller's central place theory has been re-examined and the validity of its extension into the Berry—Garrison theory of tertiary activity questioned. Likewise the use of traditional techniques for determining hierarchical groups has been critically queried and an alternative procedure, the geotaxonomic method using the frequency modulated relative homogeneity function and average member linkage, has been advocated for analysing the relationship of intra-metropolitan shopping centres on the basis of their internal structures.

The other main objective of the book was to re-examine the work of Lösch. This has been done and the manner in which his system of market areas was derived has been clarified. On the basis of this clarification Lösch's work has been blended with the earlier theories to provide a conceptual model of the location of intra-metropolitan tertiary activity that is offered as a theoretically and empirically more viable statement of actual conditions than the earlier stepped-hierarchy model.

Stolper's (1953) claim that Lösch's work opens new vistas and avenues for research has been shown to be particularly apposite. Certainly Von Böventer's (1962) contention that Lösch's economic landscape is more relevant to secondary production than to the analysis of retail and service business in the tertiary sector has been shown to be false. Clearly the next step in the extension of Lösch's work must be the welding of the structural components of the intra-urban model here presented, with Rushton's (1971) behavioural component. Only then will a unified and general theory of the intra-metropolitan tertiary activity system come closer to being a reality.

References

Abiodun, J. O., 1967: Urban hierarchy in a developing country. *Econ. Geog.*, 43, 347—67.

Abler, R., Adams, J. S. and Gould, P., 1971: *Spatial Organization: The Geographer's View of the World*, Prentice-Hall, Englewood Cliffs.

Alexander, J. W., 1963: *Economic Geography*, Prentice-Hall, Englewood Cliffs.

Allpass, J., Agergard, E., Harvest, J., Olsen, P. A. and Søholt, S., 1967: Urban centres and changes in the centre structure. In *Urban Core and Inner City*, Heinemeijer, W. F., van Hulten, M. and de Vries Reilingh, H. D. (eds.), 103—17.

Ambrose, P. (ed.), 1969: *Analytical Human Geography*, Longmans (Concepts in Geography, 2), London.

Andrews, H. F., 1970: *Working Notes and Bibliography on Central Place Studies 1965—1969*, University of Toronto (Department of Geography Discussion Paper No. 8), Toronto.

Angel, S. and Hyman, G. M., 1972: Transformations and geographic theory. *Geog. Anal.*, 4, 350—67.

Barnes, J. A. and Robinson, A. H., 1940: A new method for the representation of dispersed rural population. *Geog. Rev.*, 30, 134—7.

Barnum, H. G., 1966: *Market Centers and Hinterlands in Baden—Württemberg*, University of Chicago (Department of Geography Research Paper, No. 103), Chicago.

Barnum, H. G., Kasperson, R. and Kiuchi, S., 1965: *Supplement to Central Place Studies: A Bibliography of Theory and Applications*, Berry, B. J. L. and Pred, A. (eds.), Regional Science Research Institute (Bibliography Series No. 1), Philadelphia.

Baskin, C. W., 1957: A Critique and Translation of W. Christaller's *Die zentralen Orte in Süddeutschland*, unpublished Ph.D. thesis, University of Virginia.

Baskin, C. W., 1966: Notes in Christaller, W., 1966: *Central Places in Southern Germany*, Prentice-Hall, Englewood Cliffs.

Baumol, W. J. and Ide, E. A., 1956: Variety in retailing. *Management Science*, 3, 93—101.

Beavon, K. S. O., 1970a: *Land Use Patterns in Port Elizabeth: An Analysis in the Environs of Main Street*, A. A. Balkema, Cape Town.

Beavon, K. S. O., 1970b: An alternative approach to the classification of urban hierarchies. *S. Afr. Geog. J.*, 52, 129—33.

Beavon, K. S. O., 1972: The intra-urban continuum of shopping centres in Cape Town. *S. Afr. Geog. J.*, 54, 58—71.

Beavon, K. S. O., 1973: A procedure for constructing Lösch's regional system of markets. *S. Afr. J. Sci.*, 69, 377—9.

Beavon, K. S. O., 1974a: Interpreting Lösch on an intra-urban scale. *S. Afr. Geog. J.*, 56, 36—59.

Beavon, K. S. O., 1974b: Generalising the intra-urban model based on Lösch. *S. Afr. Geog. J.*, 56, 137—54.

Beavon, K. S. O., 1974c: *A Model of the Location of Intra-metropolitan Tertiary Activity*, unpublished Ph.D thesis, University of the Witwatersrand, Johannesburg.

Beavon, K. S. O., 1975: Christaller's central place theory: reviewed, revealed, revised. *Environmental Studies*, Department of Geography and Environmental Studies, University of the Witwatersrand (Occasional Paper 15), Johannesburg.

Beavon, K. S. O., 1976: The Lösch intra-urban model under conditions of changing cost functions. *S. Afr. Geog. J.*, 58, 36—9.

Beavon, K. S. O. and Hall, A. V., 1972: A geotaxonomic approach to classification in urban and regional systems. *Geog. Anal.*, 4, 407—15.

Beavon, K. S. O. and Mabin, A. S., 1975: The Lösch system of market areas: derivation and extension. *Geog. Anal.*, 7, 131—51.

Beavon, K. S. O. and Mabin, A. S., 1976: A pedagogic approach to the Löschian system of market areas. *Tij. Econ. Soc. Geog.*, 67, 29—37.

Beckmann, M., 1958: City hierarchies and the distribution of city size. *Econ. Dev. Cult. Chng.*, 6, 243—8.

Beckmann, M., 1970: *Discussion Paper 16*, Brown University.

Bell, T. L., Lieber, S. R. and Rushton, G., 1974: Clustering of services in central places. *Ann. Ass. Am. Geog.*, 64, 214—25.

Berry, B. J. L., 1962: *The Commercial Structure of American Cities: A Review*, Community Renewal Program, Chicago.

Berry, B. J. L., 1963: *Commercial Structure and Commercial Blight*, University of Chicago (Department of Geography Research Paper, No. 85), Chicago.

Berry, B. J. L., 1964: The case of the mistreated model. *Prof. Geog.*, 16, 15—16.

Berry, B. J. L., 1967: *Geography of Market Centers and Retail Distribution*, Prentice-Hall (Foundations of Economic Geography Series), Englewood Cliffs.

Berry, B. J. L. and Barnum, H. G., 1962: Aggregate relations and elemental components of central place systems. *J. Reg. Sci.*, 4, 35—68.

Berry, B. J. L., Barnum, H. G. and Tennant, R. J., 1962: Retail location and consumer behaviour. *Pap. Proc. Reg. Sci. Ass.*, 9, 65—106.

Berry, B. J. L. and Garrison, W. L., 1958a: Functional bases of the central place hierarchy. *Econ. Geog.*, 34, 145—54.

Berry, B. J. L. and Garrison, W. L., 1958b: A note on central place theory and the range of a good. *Econ. Geog.*, 34, 304—11.

Berry, B. J. L. and Garrison, W. L., 1958c: Recent developments of central place theory. *Pap. Proc. Reg. Sci. Ass.*, 4, 107—20.

Berry, B. J. L. and Horton, F. E., 1970: *Geographic Perspectives on Urban Systems*, Prentice-Hall, Englewood Cliffs.

Berry, B. J. L. and Pred, A., 1961: *Central Place Studies: A Bibliography of Theory and Applications*, Regional Science Research Institute (Bibliography Series No. 1), Philadelphia.

Boal, F. W. and Johnson, D. B., 1965: The functions of retail and service establishments on commercial ribbons. *Can. Geog.*, 9, 154—69.

Bollobas, B. and Stern, N. H., 1972: The optimal structure of market areas. *J. Econ. Theory*, 4, 174—9.

Bourne, L. S. (ed.), 1971: *Internal Structure of the City: Readings on Space and Environment*, Oxford University Press, London.

Bracey, H. E., 1953: Towns as rural service centres. *Trans. Pap. Inst. Brit. Geog.*, 19, 95—105.

Brundrit, G. B., 1972: Pairwise dissimilarity measures for ordinal data. Discussion paper, Department of Applied Mathematics, University of Cape Town, Rondebosch.

Brush, J. E., 1953: The hierarchy of central places in southwestern Wisconsin. *Geog. Rev.*, 43, 380—402.

Brush, J. E. and Bracey, H. E., 1955: Rural service centres in southwestern Wisconsin and southern England. *Geog. Rev.*, 45, 559—69.

Bunge, W., 1962: *Theoretical Geography*, University of Lund (Studies in Geography, C, 1), Lund.

Burton, I., 1963: The quantitative revolution and theoretical geography. *Can. Geogr.*, 7, 151—62.

Cain, A. J. and Harrison, J. A., 1958: An analysis of the taxonomic judgement of affinity. *Proc. Zoo. Soc. Lon.*, 131, 85—98.

Canoyer, H. G., 1946: *Selecting a Store Location*, Government Printing Office (United States Bureau of Foreign and Domestic Commerce, Economic Series, 56), Washington.

Carol, H., 1952: Das Agrargeographische Betrachtungssystem. Ein Beitrag zur landschafts-kundlichen Methodik dargelegt am Beispiel der in Südafrika. *Geographica Helvetica*, 1, 17—67.

Carol, H., 1960: The hierarchy of central functions within the city. *Ann. Ass. Am. Geog.*, 50, 419—38.

Carruthers, W. I., 1962: Service centres in greater London. *T. Plan Rev.*, 33, 5—31.

Carter, H., 1956: The urban hierarchy and historical geography: a consideration with reference to northeast Wales. *Geog. Stud.*, 3, 85—101.

Carter, H., 1972: *The Study of Urban Geography*, Edward Arnold, London.

Carter, H. and Davies, W. K. D. (eds.), 1970: *Urban Essays: Studies in the Geography of Wales*, Longmans, London.

Chorley, R. J. and Haggett, P. (eds.), 1967: *Models in Geography*, Methuen, London.

Christaller, W., 1933: *Die Zentralen Orte in Süddeutschland*. Fischer, Jena. English edition translated by Baskin, C. W., 1966: *Central Places in Southern Germany*, Prentice-Hall, Englewood Cliffs.

Christaller, W., 1950: Das Grundgerüst der räumlichen der Ordnung in Europa: Die Systeme der europäischen zentralen Orte. *Frankfurter Geographische Hefte*, 24, 5–14.

Christaller, W., 1960: Die hierachie der Städte. *Proc. IGU Symposium in Urban Geography, Lund 1960*, Norborg, K. (ed.) (Lund Studies in Geography B, 24), University of Lund, 3–11.

Christaller, W., 1966: *Central Places in Southern Germany* (translated by C. W. Baskin), Prentice-Hall, Englewood Cliffs.

Clark, P. J. and Evans, F. C., 1954: Distance to nearest neighbour as a measure of spatial relations. *Ecology*, 35, 445–53.

Clark, W. A. V., 1967: The spatial structure of retail functions in a New Zealand city. *N.Z. Geog.*, 23, 23–33.

Clark, W. A. V., 1968: Consumer travel patterns and the concept of range. *Ann. Ass. Am. Geog.*, 58, 386–96.

Clark, W. A. V. and Rushton, G., 1970: Models of intra-urban consumer behaviour and their implications for central place theory. *Econ. Geog.*, 49, 486–97.

Colless, D. H., 1967: An examination of certain concepts in phenetic taxonomy. *Syst. Zoo.*, 16, 6–27.

Cowie, S. R., 1968: The cumulative frequency nearest neighbour method for the identification of spatial patterns. *Seminar Papers* (Series A), 10, University of Bristol, Department of Geography, Bristol.

Curry, L., 1962: The geography of service centres within towns: the elements of an operational approach. *The IGU Symposium in Urban Geography Lund 1960*, Norborg, K. (ed.), University of Lund (Lund Studies in Geography, B, 24), Lund, 31–53.

Dacey, M. F., 1965a: An interesting number property in central place theory. *Prof. Geog.*, 17, 32–3.

Dacey, M. F., 1965b: The geometry of central place theory. *Geografiska Annaler*, 47B, 111–24.

Dacey, M. F. and Sen, A., 1968: Complete characterization of the central place hexagonal lattice. *J. Reg. Sci.*, 8, 209–13.

Davies, D. H., 1965: *Land Use in Central Cape Town*, Longman, Cape Town.

Davies, D. H. and Beavon, K. S. O., 1973: Changes in the land use patterns in central Cape Town, 1957–1964. *Environmental Studies*, University of the Witwatersrand (Department of Geography and Environmental Studies, Occasional Paper No. 10), Johannesburg.

Davies, R. J., 1967: The South African urban hierarchy. *S. Afr. Geog. J.*, 49, 9–19.

Davies, R. J. and Cook, G. P., 1968: Reappraisal of the South African urban hierarchy. *S. Afr. Geog. J.*, 50, 116–32.

Davies, R. L., 1968: Effects of consumer income differences on the business provisions of small shopping centres. *Urb. Stud.*, 5, 144–64.

Davies, R. L., 1969: Effects of consumer income differences on shopping movement behaviour. *Tij. Econ. Soc. Geog.*, 60, 111–21.

Davies, W. K., 1965: Some considerations of scale in central place analysis. *Tij. Econ. Soc. Geog.*, 56, 221–7.

Davies, W. K., 1967: Centrality and the central place hierarchy. *Urb. Stud.*, 4, 61–79.

Davies, W. K., 1968: Morphology of central places: a case study. *Ann. Ass. Am. Geog.*, 58, 91–110.

Dawson, J. A., 1969: Some early theories of settlement and location and size. *J. Roy. T. Plan. Inst.*, 55, 444–8.

Denike, K. G. and Parr, J. B., 1970: Production in space, spatial competition and restricted entry. *J. Reg. Sci.*, 10, 49–63.

Devletoglou, N. E., 1965: A dissenting view of duopoly and spatial competition. *Economica.*, 32, 140–60.

Dickinson, R. E., 1964: *City and Region: A Geographical Interpretation*, Routledge and Kegan Paul, London.

Dutt, A. K., 1969: Intra-city hierarchy of central places: Calcutta as a case study. *Prof. Geog.*, 21, 18–22.

Edwards, W., 1954: The theory of decision making. *Psycho. Bull.*, 51, 380–417.

Everson, J. A. and FitzGerald, B. P., 1972: *Inside the City*, Longman (Concepts in Geography 3), London.

Galpin, C. J., 1915: *The Social Anatomy of an Agricultural Community*, University of Wisconsin (Agricultural Experiment Station, Research Bulletin No. 34), Madison.

Garner, B. J., 1966: *The Internal Structure of Retail Nucleations*, Northwestern University (Studies in Geography 12), Evanston.

Garrison, W. L., 1950: *The Business Structure of the Consumer Tributary Area of the Fountain Square Major Outlying Business Centre of Evanston, Ill.*, unpublished Ph.D. thesis, Northwestern University, Evanston.

Garrison, W. L., Berry, B. J. L., Marble, D. F., Nystuen, J. D. and Morrill, R. L., 1959: *Studies of Highway Development and Geographic Change*, University of Washington Press, Seattle.

Getis, A. and Getis, J., 1966: Christaller's central place theory. *J. Geog.*, 220–6.

Golledge, R. G., Rushton, G. and Clark, W. A. V., 1966: Some spatial characteristics of Iowa's dispersed farm population and their implications for the grouping of central place functions. *Econ. Geog.*, 43, 261–72.

Goodall, B., 1972: *The Economics of Urban Areas*, Pergamon, Oxford.

Goodall, D. W., 1963: The continuum and the individualistic association. *Vegetatio*, 11, 297–316.

Gradmann, R., 1916: Schwäbische städte. *Zeit. Gesell. Erd.*, 427.

Gradmann, R., 1926: Das ländliche Siedlungswesen des Königreichs Würtemberg. *Forschungen zur deutschen Landes-und Volkskunde*, 21 (1), Stuttgart.

Greenhut, M. L., 1970: *A Theory of the Firm in Economic Space*, Appleton-Century-Crofts, New York.

Greenhut, M. L. and Ohta, H., 1972: The theory of spatial prices and market areas. Unpublished manuscript, cited by Hartwick, 1973.

Grigg, D., 1965: The logic of regional systems. *Ann. Ass. Am Geog.*, 55, 465–91.

Hägerstrand, T., 1965: A Monte Carlo approach to diffusion. *Eur. J. Socio.*, 6, 43–67.

Haggett, P., 1965: *Locational Analysis in Human Geography*, Edward Arnold, London.

Haggett, P., 1972: *Geography: A Modern Synthesis*, Harper and Row, New York.

Hall, A. V., 1967: Methods for demonstrating resemblance in taxonomy and ecology. *Nature (Lond.)*, 214, 830–1.

Hall, A. V., 1969a: Avoiding informational distortions in automatic grouping programs. *Syst. Zoo.*, 18, 318–29.

Hall, A. V., 1969b: Group forming and discrimination with homogeneity functions, in Cole, A. J. (ed.), *Numerical Taxonomy*, Academic Press, London, 53–68.

Hamilton, F. E. I., 1967: Models of industrial location. In *Models in Geography*, Chorley, R. J. and Haggett, P. (eds.), 361–424.

Hartwick, J. M., 1970: Lösch's theorem of hexagonal market areas. *Discussion Paper No. 25*, Queens University, Toronto.

Hartwick, J. M., 1973: Lösch's theorem on hexagonal market areas. *Jour. Reg. Sci.*, 13, 213–21.

Heinemeijer, W. F., van Hulten, M. and de Vries Reilingh, H. D. (eds.), 1967: *Urban Core and Inner City: Proceedings of the International Study Week Amsterdam, September 1966* (University of Amsterdam Sociographical Department), Brill, Leiden.

Henderson, J. V., 1972: Hierarchy models of city size: an economic evaluation. *J. Reg. Sci.*, 12, 435–41.

Holton, R. H., 1957: Price discrimination at retail: the supermarket case. *J. Ind. Econ.*, 6, 13–32.

Horvath, R. J., 1969: Von Thünen's isolated state and the area around Addis Ababa, Ethiopia. *Ann. Ass. Am. Geog.*, 59, 308–23.

Hudson, J. C., 1967: An algebraic relation between the Lösch and Christaller central place networks. *Prof. Geog.*, 19, 133–5.

Huff, D. L., 1962: *Determination of Intra-urban Retail Trade Areas*, University of California (Los Angeles Real Estate Program), Los Angeles.

Hurst, M. E., 1972: *A Geography of Economic Behavior*, Duxberry Press, North Scituate, Mass.

Isard, W., 1956: *Location and Space Economy*, MIT Press, Cambridge, Mass.

Jefferson, M., 1931: The distribution of the world's city folks. *Geog. Rev.*, 21, 446–65.

Johnson, J. H., 1967: *Urban Geography: An Introductory Analysis*, Pergamon, Oxford.

Johnston, R. J., 1964: The measurement of a hierarchy of central places. *Austrl. Geog.*, 9, 315–17.

Johnston, R. J., 1966: The distribution of an intra-metropolitan central place hierarchy. *Austrl. Geog. Stud.*, 4, 19—33.

Johnston, R. J., 1968a: Choice in classification: the subjectivity of objective methods. *Ann. Ass. Am. Geog.*, 58, 575—89.

Johnston, R. J., 1968b: Railways, urban growth and central place patterns: an example from south-east Melbourne. *Tij. Econ. Soc. Geog.*, 59, 33—41.

Johnston, R. J., 1970: Grouping and regionalizing: some methodological and technical observations. *Econ. Geog.*, 46, 293—305.

Johnston, R. J. and Rimmer, P. J., 1967a: A note on consumer behaviour in an urban hierarchy. *J. Reg. Sci.*, 7, 161—6.

Johnston, R. J. and Rimmer, P. J., 1967b: The competitive position of a planned shopping centre. *Austrl. Geog.*, 5, 160—8.

Joint Town Planning Committee, 1955: *Provisional Joint Town Planning Scheme of the First Section: Preliminary Statement, March 1949* (amended 1950, 1955), City Engineer's Department, Cape Town.

King, L. J., 1962: The fundamental role of small towns in Canterbury. *Proc. Third N.Z. Geog. Conf., Palmerston North*, 139—49.

Kohl, J. G., 1850: *Der Verkeur und die Ansiedelungen der Menschen in ihrer Abhängigkeit von der Gestaltung der Erdoberflache* (2nd edn), Leipzig.

Kolb, J. H., 1923: *Service Relations of Town and Country*, University of Wisconsin (Agricultural Experimental Station, Research Bulletin No. 58), Madison.

Kolb, J. H. and Brunner, E. de S., 1946: *A Study of Rural Society*, W. F. Ogburn (ed.), Houghton Mifflin, New York.

Kolb, J. H. and Polson, R. A., 1933: *Trends in Town—Country Relations*, University of Wisconsin (Agricultural Experiment Station, Research Bulletin No. 117), Madison.

Kuenne, R. E., 1963: *The Theory of General Economic Equilibrium*, Princeton University Press, Princeton.

Labovitz, S., 1968: Criteria for selecting a significance level: a note on the sacredness of .05. *Am. Socio.*, 3, 220—2.

Lakshmanan, T. R. and Hansen, W. G., 1965: A retail market potential model. *J. Am. Inst. Plan.*, 31, 134—43.

Lalanne, L., 1863: Les villes et les routes. *Comptes rendus de l'Académie des Sciences.*

Lambert, J. M. and Dale, M. B., 1964: The use of statistics in phytosociology. *Advances in Ecological Research*, 2, 59—99.

Leahy, W. H., McKee, D. L. and Dean, R. D. (eds.), 1970: *Urban Economics: Theory Development and Planning*, The Free Press, New York.

Lewis, C. R., 1970: The central place pattern of Mid-Wales and the middle Welsh borderland. In *Urban Essays: Studies in the Geography of Wales*, Carter, H. and Davies, W. K. D. (eds.), 228—68.

Lipsey, R. G., 1966: *An Introduction to Positive Economics* (2nd edn), Weidenfeld and Nicolson, London.

Lloyd, P. E. and Dicken, P., 1972: *Location in Space: A Theoretical Approach to Economic Geography*, Harper and Row, New York.

Lomas, G. M., 1964: Retail trade centres in the Midlands. *J. Roy. T. Plan. Inst.*, 50, 104—19.

Lösch, A., 1943: *Die räumliche Ordnung der Wirtschaft: eine Untersuchung über Standort, Wirtschaftgebiete und internationalen Handel*, Fischer, Jena. English translation by Woglom, W. H., 1954: *The Economics of Location*, Yale University Press, New Haven.

Machiavelli, N., 1531: *The Discourses on the First Decade of Titus Livius* (translated by L. J. Walker), London, 1950 (as cited by Dawson, 1969).

McEvoy, D., 1968: Alternative methods of ranking shopping centres. *Tij. Econ. Soc. Geog.*, 59, 211—17.

McQuitty, L. L., 1957: Elementary linkage analysis for isolating orthogonal and oblique types and typal relevancies. *Ed. Psycho. Measurement*, 17, 207—29.

March, J. G. and Simon, H. A., 1958: *Organizations*, Wiley, New York.

Marshall, J. U., 1964: Model and reality in central place studies. *Prof. Geog.*, 16, 5—8.

Marshall, J. U., 1969: *The Location of Service Towns*, University of Toronto (Department of Geography Research Publication No. 3), Toronto.

Mayer, H. M. and Kohn, C. F. (eds.), 1959: *Readings in Urban Geography*, University of Chicago Press, Chicago.

Mills, E. S. and Lav, M. R., 1964: A model of market areas with free entry. *J. Pol. Econ.*, 72, 278—88.

Mitchell, R. A., Lentnek, B. and Osleeb, J. P., 1974: Towards a dynamic theory of central places. *Discussion Paper No. 41*, Department of Geography, Ohio State University, Columbus.

Morrill, R. L., 1970: *The Spatial Organization of Society*, Wadsworth, Belmont, Calif.

Muller, P. O. and Diaz, G. J., 1973: Von Thünen and population density. *Prof. Geog.*, 25, 239–41.

Murphy, R. E., 1966: *The American City: An Urban Geography*, McGraw-Hill, New York.

Nelson, R. L., 1958: *The Selection of Retail Locations*, Dodge Corp., New York.

Olsson, G., 1965: *Distance and Human Interaction: A Review and Bibliography*, Regional Science Research Institute (Bibliography Series No. 2), Philadelphia.

Palomäki, M., 1964: The functional centres and areas of South Bothnia Finland. *Fennia*, 88, 1–235.

Parr, J. B., 1973: Structure and size in the urban system of Lösch. *Econ. Geog.*, 49, 185–212.

Parr, J. B. and Denike, K. G., 1970: Theoretical problems in central place analysis. *Econ. Geog.*, 46, 568–86.

Pownall, L. L., 1955: *The Contemporary New Zealand Town*, unpublished Ph.D. thesis, University of New Zealand.

Pred. A., 1966: *The Spatial Dynamics of the U.S. Urban–Industrial Growth 1800–1914: Interpretative and Theoretical Essays*, MIT Press, Cambridge, Mass.

Preston, R. E., 1971: Towards a verification of a 'classical' centrality model. *Tij. Econ. Soc. Geog.*, 62, 301–7.

Proudfoot, M. J., 1937: City retail structure. *Econ. Geog.*, 13, 425–8.

Rao, C. R., 1948: The utilisation of multiple measurement in problems of biological classification. *J. Roy. Stat. Soc.*, B, 10, 187–8.

Ratcliff, R. U., 1949: *Urban Land Economics*, McGraw-Hill, New York.

Reilly, W. J., 1931: *The Law of Retail Gravitation*, Knickerbocker Press, New York.

Robinson, K., 1968: *Central Place Theory II: Its Role in Planning with Particular Reference to Retailing*, Centre for Environmental Studies (Working Paper No. 9), London.

Rolph, I. K., 1929: *The Location Structure of Retail Trade*, The Government Printing Office (United States Bureau of Foreign and Domestic Commerce, Domestic Commerce Series, 80), Washington.

Rowley, G., 1970: Central places in rural Wales: a case study. *Tij. Econ. Soc. Geog.*, 61, 32–41.

Rowley, G., 1972: Spatial variations in the prices of central goods. *Tij. Econ. Soc. Geog.*, 63, 360–8.

Rushton, G., 1969a: Analysis of spatial behavior by revealed space preference. *Ann. Ass. Am. Geog.*, 59, 391–400.

Rushton, G., 1969b: The scaling of locational preferences. In Cox, K. and Golledge, R. G. (eds.), *Problems of Behavioural Geography*, Northwestern University (Studies in Geography 17), 197–227.

Rushton, G., 1969c: Temporal changes in space preference structures. *Proc. Ass. Am. Geog.*, 1, 129–32.

Rushton, G., 1971: Postulates of central place theory and the properties of central place systems. *Geog. Anal.*, 3, 140–56.

Rushton, G., 1972: Map transformations of point patterns: central place patterns in areas of variable population density. *Reg. Sci. Ass. Pap.*, 28, 111–29.

Rushton, G., Golledge, R. G. and Clark, W. A. V., 1967: Formulation and test of a normative model for the spatial allocation of grocery expenditures by a dispersed population. *Ann. Ass. Am. Geog.*, 57, 389–400.

Saey, P., 1973: Three fallacies in the literature on central place theory. *Tij. Econ. Soc. Geog.*, 64, 181–94.

Scott, P., 1964: The hierarchy of central places in Tasmania. *Austrl. Geog.*, 9, 134–47.

Simmons, J. W., 1964: *The Changing Pattern of Retail Location*, University of Chicago (Department of Geography Research Paper No. 92), Chicago.

Simmons, J. W., 1966: *Toronto's Changing Retail Complex: A Study in Growth and Blight*, University of Chicago (Department of Geography Research Paper No. 104), Chicago.

Smailes, A. E., 1944: The urban hierarchy in England and Wales. *Geog.*, 29, 41–51.

Spence, N. A. and Taylor, P. J., 1970: Quantitative methods in regional taxonomy. In Board, C., Chorley, R. J., Haggett, P. and Stoddart, D. R. (eds.), *Progress in Geography*, No. 2, Arnold, London, 1–64.

Stern, N. H., 1972: The optimal size of market areas. *J. Econ. Theory.*, 4, 154–73.

Stolper, W. F., 1953: August Lösch in Memoriam. In Lösch, 1954.

Stolper, W. F., 1955: Spatial order and the economic growth of cities. *Econ. Dev. Cult. Chng.*, 3, 137—46.

Tarrant, J. R., 1973: Comments on the Lösch central place system. *Geog. Anal.*, 5, 113—21.

Thoman, R. S., Conkling, E. C. and Yeates, M. H., 1968: *The Geography of Economic Activity* (2nd edn), McGraw-Hill, New York.

Thomas, E. N., Mitchell, R. A. and Blome, D. A., 1962: The spatial behavior of a dispersed non-farm population. *Pap. Proc. Reg. Sci. Ass.*, 9, 107—33.

Tobler, W. R., 1963: Geographic area and map projections. *Geog. Rev.*, 53, 59—78.

Tobler, W. R., 1970: *Selected Computer Programs*, Department of Geography, Ann Arbor, Michigan.

Trewartha, G. T., 1943: The unincorporated hamlet: one element of the American settlement fabric. *Ann. Ass. Am. Geog.*, 33, 32—81.

Ullman, E., 1941: A theory of location for cities. *Am. J. Socio.*, 46, 835—64.

Valavanis, S., 1955: Lösch on location. *Am. Econ. Rev.*, 45, 637—44.

Vining, R., 1955: A description of certain spatial aspects of an economic system. *Ec. Dev. Cult, Chng.*, 3, 147—95.

Von Böventer, E., 1962: Towards a unified theory of spatial economic structure. *Pap. Proc. Reg. Sci. Ass.*, 10, 163—87.

Vrišer, I., 1971: The pattern of central places in Yugoslavia. *Tij. Econ. Soc. Geog.*, 62, 290—300.

Walmsley, D. J., 1974: Retail spatial structure in suburban Sydney. *Austrl. Geog.*, 12, 401—18.

Webber, M. J., 1972: *Impact of Uncertainty on Location*, MIT Press, Cambridge, Mass.

Wehrwein, G. S., 1942: The rural urban fringe. *Econ. Geog.*, 18, 217—28.

Yeates, M. H. and Garner, B. J., 1971: *The North American City*, Harper and Row, New York.

Index of authors

Index of subjects